Saturday Sunday Monday

A PLAY IN THREE ACTS

by *Eduardo de Filippo*

English Adaptation

by *Keith Waterhouse & Willis Hall*

D1096662

SAMUEL FRENCH, INC.

45 WEST 25TH STREET   NEW YORK 10010

7623 SUNSET BOULEVARD HOLLYWOOD 90046

LONDON   TORONTO

Keith Waterhouse and Willis Hall

ALL RIGHTS RESERVED

ISBN 0 573 61513-6   Printed in U.S.A.

SATURDAY, SUNDAY, MONDAY by Eduardo de Filippo, was first performed in the U.S. at the Martin Beck Theatre, New York City, on November 21, 1974. The play was produced by Barry M. Brown, Fritz Holt and S. Spencer Davids by arrangement with The National Theatre of Great Britain. English adaptation by Keith Waterhouse and Willis Hall. Directed and designed by Franco Zeffrelli, lighting by Roger Morgan, original National Theatre costume designs by Raimonda Gaetani and hairstyles by Ted Azar.

CHARACTERS

THE FAMILY:

ANTONIO .... *Walter Abel*

ROSA .... *Sada Thompson*
PEPPINO .... *Eli Wallach*
MARIA .... *Susan Merson*
ROBERTO .... *William McCauley*
ROCCO .... *Jeff Giannone*
GIULIANELLA .... *Francesca Bartoccini*

AUNT MEME .... *Jan Miner*
ATTILIO .... *Amos Abrams*

RAFFAELE .... *Michael Vale*

AND:

VIRGINIA, the maid ...... *Minnie Gordon Gaster*
FEDERICO, Giulianella's fiance ...... *Gary Sandy*
LUIGI IANNIELLO, the accountant .. *Ron Holgate*
ELENA, his wife .... *Nina Dova*
CATIELLO, the tailor .... *Michael Enserro*
MICHELE .... *Terry Hinz*
DR. CEFERCOLA .... *Sam Gray*

3

ACT ONE

Saturday

ACT TWO

Sunday

ACT THREE

Monday

TIME: The Present

PLACE: The Priore Family's Apartment in Naples

Saturday, Sunday, Monday

ACT ONE

DONNA ROSA *stands at the kitchen stove—Upstage end—stirring the soup in a pot on the Upstage burner.* VIRGINIA, *the maid, is slicing onions. Every so often, the girl has to wipe her eyes, but she continues bravely.*

ROSA. (*She crosses to sink, gets plate of parsley.*) Haven't you finished yet?

VIRGINIA. Nearly. Only two more.

ROSA. (*She brings plate to table.*) Hurry up— I'm waiting.

VIRGINIA. Signora, I think I've done enough already.

ROSA. Are you telling me how to make *ragu?* The more onions there are, the thicker the sauce. I'll tell you how to make *ragu,* it's all in the cooking. Slowly, over a low flame. Then the onions curl up round the meat in a black crust. When you add the white wine, the crust loosens. That makes a rich golden stock and then you mix it with the tomato sauce and that gives it that lovely dark colour. *Ragu* shouldn't only taste right, it should look right. Don't you try tell me how to make *ragu!* (*She gets scissors and string from left drawer of table.*)

VIRGINIA. At home we just fry the onions, put in the tomatoes and meat and boil it all up together.

ROSA. I am sure you do . . . And what does it taste like? Boiled meat with tomatoes and onions! My mother would have told you how to make *ragu.* "To make a *ragu,*" she used to say, "takes patience." And she had some patience, my mama! Every Saturday

5

night she was in the kitchen— (*She picks up ladle.*) the ladle in her hand. At this very table. And nothing would make her move away from her casserole dish— if a murderer climbed in through the window she would not move. When it was half-cooked in the casserole dish, she would tip it out and finish it off in the big pot. (*She gets pot from wall above sink and returns to table.*) There was no aluminium in those days. When the sauce was ready—just at the right moment—the meat was taken out of the casserole dish and placed in the big pot— (*She lifts meat from Left chopping board, puts it on oval platter.*) carefully, like a newborn babe in its cradle. My mother knew how to make *ragu* all right! (*She goes to sink, picks up pot lid from work area Left of sink.*)

VIRGINIA. (*Politely.*) Of course, if you have a passion for cooking.

ROSA. And my father, you know what Don Antonio is like—if his Sunday *ragu* wasn't fit to be confessed and blessed, oh! The house wasn't worth living in. (*She takes lid to stove and puts it on Stage side of stove, between Downstage burners.*)

VIRGINIA. Your poor mama!

ROSA. She worshipped him. And you know why? Because he worshipped her *ragu.* (*She fans fire, Center door.*) Friends would stop her in the street. "Signora," they'd say, "What's the recipe for the *ragu* that your husband never stops talking about?" It was always, "My wife's *ragu* this" and "My wife's *ragu* that." Mama would ask him to bring his friends and their wives round to Sunday dinner. (*She fans fire, Upstage door.*) Afterwards they would say: "He's right, your husband. The *ragu's* wonderful!" And, as they went out, they would cross themselves.

VIRGINIA. It's a pity your husband hasn't much of an appetite.

ROSA. (*Stirs soup.*) Don Peppino does not show enthusiasm for food—he's above that sort of thing. If

i was just for my husband's sake I'd give him yester-
(y's macaroni, even on Easter Sunday—he wouldn't
notice. (*She notices that* VIRGINIA's *face is marked by
tears and that the girl is sobbing heavily.* ROSA *crosses
Right to table.*) Is that the onion or are you really
crying?

VIRGINIA. I'm really crying, Signora. (*She sits down
and bursts into a fresh stream of tears.*)

ROSA. What for? What's happened to you?

VIRGINIA. It's my brother, Michele.

ROSA. What's he done?

VIRGINIA. This morning he went to get his hair cut!
And they'll arrest him again and put him away in
prison!

ROSA. Because a man has his hair cut he is arrested
and sent to prison?

VIRGINIA. An ordinary man, no, signora! My
brother, yes! (PEPPINO *wearing top coat and carrying
briefcase enters Up Left as* ROSA *stares at* VIRGINIA,
perplexed. PEPPINO, ROSA's *husband, is a man in late
middle-age, sturdy and in good health. Unaware of the
drama that is taking place, he remains near the door
examining a door key closely.*) I have to bear my
brother like a cross. (*She rises and goes Up Right.*)

PEPPINO. My son has a very strange sense of humour.
His great joke is to leave his front door key on the hall
table and take mine instead. So I go off with his key
in my pocket. (*He crosses above* ROSA *to table.*) When
I come home in the evening I spend half an hour
fiddling in the keyhole. Very funny! He does it on
purpose—because his key doesn't fit properly and mine
does.

ROSA. (*She crosses Right above* PEPPINO *to* VIRGINIA.
In irritation.) Excuse me, I'm trying to listen to Virginia.

PEPPINO. What's the matter?

ROSA. (*Without deigning to look at him.*) She's crying, can't you see?

PEPPINO. (*He crosses Left.*) We're not on the same wave length, are we, you and I? I can see that she's crying. I'm asking—why?

ROSA. I'm trying to find that out. (*She leads VIR-GINIA to Right of table. ROSA sits above table.*) Now then, your brother has his hair cut—and then? (*She puts chopper in VIRGINIA's hands, then ROSA cuts garlic and VIRGINIA chops onions.*)

VIRGINIA. Signora, it was a long time ago. He was in an accident. He was in the hospital, in and out, in and out, and when they finally sent him home he was not the same man.

ROSA. Well, what does the doctor say?

VIRGINIA. The doctor has said that there is nothing to be done. "He has this animal strength so like any other animal, he must find an outlet for that strength."

(PEPPINO *sits in chair Left of table.*)

ROSA. What sort of an outlet?

VIRGINIA. He used to push a piano up and down the road. Now it's this business of getting a hair cut. And when he gets his haircut, he's like the hammer of God.

ROSA. Virgi, I still don't understand. Stop crying and tell us.

VIRGINIA. He has the barber shave off all his hair . . . completely. And he pulls a cap down over his head.

PEPPINO. What good does that do him?

VIRGINIA. (*She crosses Left above ROSA.*) Then he goes out in the streets. When he sees a man as big as himself he stands in front of him, takes off his cap and stares him in the face. (PEPPINO *and* ROSA *laugh.*) Who wouldn't laugh? And Michele grabs him by both lapels with his two big hands and says, "You, what are you laughing at?" There is a fight. (*She returns Right above ROSA.*) Michele always wins. My brother can fill a hospital in less than a day.

ROSA. My God . . . and this morning he saw a barber? (*She rises puts lard into big pot. Takes pot and ladle to stove.*)

PEPPINO. God help everyone out in the streets!

VIRGINIA. Donna Rosa . . . ?

ROSA. What do you want?

VIRGINIA. If I could have tomorrow off . . . (*She crosses Left.*) he never so much as lifts a finger when he's with me.

ROSA. Virgi, tomorrow is Sunday. We have people coming to dinner.

PEPPINO. What people?

(VIRGINIA *goes back to table and puts chopped onions from board onto onion plate.*)

ROSA. "What people!" Relatives. Your daughter-in-law.

PEPPINO. *My* daughter-in-law.

ROSA. I apologize. I must remember to mind my grammar. *Our* daughter-in-law. Roberto and Maria Carolina.

PEPPINO. All right, all right!

ROSA. She telephoned this morning. "Mama, tomorrow is Sunday. Could we come to dinner with you?" That girl has never learned to cook.

PEPPINO. We go often enough to eat with them.

ROSA. (*She crosses to table.*) To *eat*, yes. To eat Sunday dinner, no. I know what I'm saying. Roberto would rather eat Sunday *ragu* here. (*She puts parsley on top of plate of onions that* VIRGINIA *is holding.*)

PEPPINO. You think Roberto thinks about tomorrow's ragu. He's wrapped up in his contracts and his projects. Besides, Maria Carolina is a very good cook.

ROSA. (*Pause. Not wishing to argue further.*) It isn't important—we won't talk about it any more. (*Goes to stove with plate of onions and parsley. Puts plate on Downstage end of stove.*)

VIRGINIA. (*She crosses Left to stove.*) And can I have tomorrow off, Signora?

ROSA. You want me to give you tomorrow off because you have a brother who acts like a clown? (*She crosses to table below* VIRGINIA.) I've told you that we've got company tomorrow. (*She crosses to stove with lard drippings, puts them in pot, puts empty bowl between Center and Downstage burner.*) More company. We're having Ianniello, the accountant, and his wife. (VIRGINIA *crosses to sink above* ROSA. *She then gets Right chopping board from table.*)

PEPPINO. (*Rises.*) I wait all week to have Sunday dinner with my family and you invite strangers to the table! (*He crosses Down Right below table to Down Right chair, takes off coat, leaves it on chair.*)

ROSA. (*She puts onions in pot.*) Strangers who have lived in the same block of flats as we have almost all of our married life! A year ago and this stranger was the best friend that you had in the world. (*She crosses to table with empty onion plate, scrapes garlic onto plate.*)

PEPPINO. It just so happens I do not like Ianniello anymore, that's all. He's a bore. And his wife. She's a bore. You have invited for dinner tomorrow not one bore, but two bores! (*Crosses to chair Right of table and sits.*)

ROSA. Look, I met her on the stairs. At four o'clock this afternoon. (*She crosses to stove with onion plate which now has garlic slivers on it. Puts garlic in pot.*) She was coming downstairs, I was going up. She had a present for me. One evening I had happened to mention to her that turquoise was my favorite color. She saw this— (*She wipes onion from chopping bag into garbage can Right of sink.*) turquoise cardigan, in my size, and she bought it for me. (*She crosses to table with empty plate. Puts it down on table. Picks up oil.*) So, she gave me the cardigan on the stairs. I was carrying the meat for tomorrow's *ragu*, I showed it to her— (VIRGINIA *stops working and watches* ROSA *and* PEPPINO.)

PEPPINO. She told you that nobody can make a *ragu* as well as you, that the wooden ladle is like magic in your hands, she flattered you, and you jumped up and down with delight and invited them to dinner.

ROSA. (*She puts oil on table. A sudden gust of violent anger.*) And what if I was flattered? And what if I did jump up and down—that's me! And I don't have to apologise for what I do, not to you, not to anyone! Do you want to see me jump up and down now? Do you want to see me take the *ragu* in the dish, and throw it all over the floor! (*She picks up oil and crosses to stove. Adds on to pot; puts oil can rear of stove.*)

PEPPINO. And you say that I have changed over the past year. What have you become? A female jack-in-the-box. You open a lid and out jumps a she-devil. (VIRGINIA *puts chopping board on floor Right of sink.*)

ROSA. Open your lid, Peppino, and nothing jumps out. Unless you want to pay compliments to other people who don't deserve it. (*She stirs sauce.*)

PEPPINO. I don't know what you're talking about. (VIRGINIA *wipes chopper and knife.*)

ROSA. You don't know what I'm talking about.

PEPPINO. Let's not discuss it any more. This arguing. Rosa, we have three children—

ROSA. (*She crosses to table with ladle, puts ladle on table.*) Listen to that— I would never have known.

PEPPINO. Has Rocco come home yet?

ROSA. No. (*She moves Left chopping board to Center table, takes meat off platter and puts it on board.*)

PEPPINO. What's the time now?

ROSA. (*Glancing over the clock on Right wall Downstage of* ANTONIO's *table.*) It's stopped.

VIRGINIA. (*She comes to* ROSA's *Left.*) It must be five—just after five.

ROSA. (*She gives ladle to* VIRGINIA, *who goes to stove.*

Rosa *puts bacon on meat.*) It's getting to be a habit—
leaving the shop in the hands of the salesmen and the
shop assistants.

PEPPINO. Why not, as long as you trust the cashier.

Rosa. (*She punches holes in meat.*) Why not? And
in the meantime the cashier has sold his little car and
bought a big one.

PEPPINO. If we carry on like this, in a few months
he'll be able to buy a Ferrari.

Rosa. What a business! (*She mimes putting garlic
into holes in meat.*)

PEPPINO. I have given my life to that shop. I was
always the first one there and the last one out. I used
to pull down the shutters and lock the doors myself—
and open up. (PEPPINO *crosses Down Right, gets slips
from briefcase.*) These days I've been having second
thoughts. I have come to the point when I don't care
any more. I'm a bit like the donkey, you know, who
draws the wine and drinks the water. I suppose I expected more from Rocco. He used to work well behind
the counter. Rocco was a good salesman, it's not easy.
It's not as easy as people think. He got on well with
the customers. He could sell them anything: last
year's shirt, last year's ties and send the customer
away satisfied. These days he walks in there as if there
was a smell under his nose. The shop is too old-
fashioned for him now. The customers are too old-
fashioned. I am too old-fashioned. You can't argue
with him. It's an old-fashioned shop. As long as you
make a sale—what's wrong with being old-fashioned?
We rely upon a solid suburban clientele. (PEPPINO *sits
Right of table.*) It's safe, it's sure, what's wrong with
that? Rocco has set his heart on opening his own business. For the fashionable set. In the Via Calabritto.
He thinks the fashionable set is just sitting there, waiting for him to open up. He could be wrong. I tell you,
I'm sick of the shop.

ROSA. Is that why you leave the shop early every afternoon?

PEPPINO. Let's say it's one of many reasons.

ROSA. (*She rises, crosses to stove with meat on oval platter. Leaves platter Downstage end of stove.*) Sell the shop, close down, why bother?

PEPPINO. That is probably what I'm going to do.

ROSA. (*Turns to him.*) What?

VIRGINIA. (*She comes to Right of* ROSA.) Signora Rosa, may I have tomorrow off?

ROSA. (*She crosses to table below* VIRGINIA.) Virgi, how many times? After Mass you will come straight here.

VIRGINIA. (*She follows* ROSA.) You can't expect me to work when my mind is somewhere else.

ROSA. (*She gets garlic bowl, takes it to stove above* VIRGINIA. *Leaves bowl Center edge of stove.*) Virgi, you'll be here tomorrow, with your mind, or I'll dismiss you and your mind there on the spot.

VIRGINIA. (*She crosses back Left to* ROSA.) Donna Rosa, just for tomorrow only, can't I bring my brother with me?

ROSA. (*She crosses to table above* VIRGINIA, *gets wine.* VIRGINIA *follows.*) Virgi, tomorrow is Sunday and on Sunday I want to be able to rest easy in my own home. (*She crosses back to stove with wine, backing* VIRGINIA *Left.* PEPPINO *laughs unbelievingly.*)

VIRGINIA. We can put him in the ironing room. When he's with me, he's like a lamb.

ROSA. Virgi, we'll talk about it tomorrow.

VIRGINIA. (*She crosses Right below table to above table.*) I'll bring him tomorrow and we'll talk about it.

(*Before* ROSA *can reply,* ROCCO *enters up Left with his friend,* FEDERICO. VIRGINIA *takes Left chopping board with onion plate, bacon plate. Piece of lemon, piece of string to sink.*)

Rocco. Buona sera. (*He goes over to his mother at the stove and kisses her.*)

Federico. Nice to see you, Signora Rosa.

Rosa. Buona sera, Federico.

Federico. (*He crosses Right to above table.*) Buona sera, Cavaliere. (Virginia *takes chopping board from table to sink.*)

Peppino. Buona sera to you.

Rocco. Mmmmm! Smell that! Tomorrow's *ragu* is on its way! (*He crosses below table to* Federico.) Make sure that it's a good one— I've invited Federico for dinner tomorrow. Last week I ate at his place and his mother's *ragu* was superb!

Federico. Grazie!

Rosa. (*She puts garlic in pot, stack's empty garlic bowl and empty lard dripping bowl and leaves them between Downstage and Center burner.*) Then he has my sympathy, tomorrow he'll have to be content with mine.

Federico. I'm sure it's perfect, Signora Rosa. But I can't accept the invitation— I've already promised someone I'll be somewhere else.

Rocco. (*He crosses Left above* Federico, *pushes him into chair above table.*) Federico, tomorrow you'll eat here! (*To* Rosa.) He's had another fight with Giulianella.

Rosa. Why do Sundays always start to go wrong on Saturday night?

Rocco. Giulianella's a stupid child and Federico's completely in the right.

Rosa. (*She crosses to sink.*) Rocco, don't interfere in things which don't concern you. (*She takes cup from area Left of sink, fills it with water.*)

Rocco. (*He moves Upstage.*) I wouldn't interfere in anything. Federico's upset and all I want is for the two of them to have the chance to straighten things out.

Federico. Straighten things out . . .

ROSA. (*She breaks down to* FEDERICO's *Right.*)
Federico's always welcome, but not to straighten
things out with Giulianella in front of all the family.
(*She crosses Downstage of* ROCCO *to stove with cup
of water.* ROCCO *follows* ROSA. ROSA *pours water into
pot, puts empty cup on stack of bowls.*) Why not?
Reasonably and fairly in front of impartial witnesses.

ROSA. Impartial. You've just called your sister
stupid—does that make you impartial?

ROCCO. Everybody knows what's wrong with
Giulianella—she's stupid.

FEDERICO. Rocco, she's not . . .

ROCCO. It's not entirely her fault. It's those stupid
idiots she calls her friends. Telling her that she is
beautiful, putting ideas into her head, making her
believe that she is something that she's not.

ROSA. (*She stirs pot at stove.*) Rocco, why don't
you just keep out of it?

ROCCO. (*He takes few steps to* ROSA.) Because,
mama, I happen to hold the key to the situation.

PEPPINO. It isn't the only key you happen to be
holding. (*He holds out the front door key he came in
with.*) Here, take this and give me back my own. I
don't want to lose half an hour fiddling at the keyhole
every time I come into my own home!

ROCCO. (*He crosses Right to above table.*) I didn't
do it on purpose. (*He takes his key from his pocket
and gives it to* PEPPINO. *He takes key from* PEPPINO.)

PEPPINO. It isn't the first time it has happened. (*He
examines the key.*) This isn't mine either! This is the
key we had made for my sister the first time she lost
the last one.

(ROCCO *and* PEPPINO *exchange keys again.* ROSA *takes
meat off platter and hides it Upstage of pot. Holds
lid in one hand while covering meat with cloth.*
ROSA *fans fire.*)

Rocco. Then Aunt Meme must have taken yours by mistake when she went out—and I must have taken hers.

PEPPINO. (*He rises, crosses Right with papers, puts them in briefcase.*) Everybody takes everybody's else's things—nobody takes his own! Keys, matches, toothpaste, soap! There is no respect for personal property any more! (*Calls.*) Virgi! Virginia! (*Takes clock off wall. He crosses Left below table.*) When my sister comes home, would you ask her for my key and then bring it to me?

VIRGINIA. Very well.

ROSA. You could ask her yourself.

PEPPINO. And listen to her talk about her dead husband for half an hour? Thank you, no.

ROSA. It's good that she remembers him.

PEPPINO. She talked the poor man into his grave— at least let him lie there in peace now. (*He opens Upstage Left door and is about to go out.*)

Rocco. (*He crosses to* PEPPINO.) Papa, why don't you come and see me on the Via Calabritto on Monday?

PEPPINO. Why don't I come and do what?

Rocco. The builders have nearly finished. By the end of next week I will have the decorators in. It will soon be time to fix an opening date for the shop. I thought you might be able to give me the benefit of your advice.

PEPPINO. The shop is built, the decorating is decided on, the opening date is almost fixed—and now you think you might benefit from my advice? (ROSA *stacks platter, lard drippings bowl, garlic bowl cup.*)

Rocco. I thought you might like to drop by and see how things are going.

PEPPINO. Thank you. I'll see how things are going when I come to the opening. (*He goes out, Up Left carrying the clock.*)

Rocco. If we stand on our own two feet we're wrong, if we have ideas of our own it is wrong, and we're wrong if we run to him all the time! (*He crosses Right above table.*) When I open the shop he won't even come. If he had his way I'd spend the rest of my life behind the counter of his museum in Rettifilo. (Rosa *stirs pots, fans fires.*) "I'll see how it goes on the opening!" He'll see how it's going in six months when everybody in Naples is coming to me. And that place of his is even more run down than it is now! (*Sits Right of table.*)

Rosa. You mind the way you speak about your father—or you'll feel my hand across your face!

Rocco. Mama— I'm grown up. I have hands too.

Rosa. (*She crosses to Left end of table.*) What was that? What did you say?

Rocco. It was only a joke.

Rosa. I don't like those kind of jokes. "Mama, I have hands too." I know you have hands. I *gave* you hands. (Rocco *rises and moves below table to* Rosa.) To work, as your father has worked all his life. If you are too clever for your father, you are too clever for your mother too.

Rocco. Mama, please . . .

Rosa. (*She slaps his hands.*) Take your hands, Rocco, and use them to open the door. (*She crosses Left to stove.*)

Rocco. Don't you want me to say I'm sorry?

Rosa. (*She crosses Right to table.*) Rocco, I want you to go!

Rocco. But mama . . .

Rosa. Now, get out! Or I'll hit you with a plate. (*She has snatched up several plates from the table and is holding them threateningly.*)

Rocco. Mama, this is going too far!

Federico. (*He rises, grabs plates.*) Signora Rosa, Rocco didn't really mean what he said.

Rosa. Perhaps not. But Rocco knows that *I* always mean what I say. (*She crosses Left to stove.* Federico *puts plates on table as* Rosa *crosses Left.*)

Rocco. (*He crosses above table.*) Federico, it would be better for all concerned if I go.

Rosa. Better for who?

Rocco. For me! Better for me, Mama, I am agreeing with you! Federi, do you want to stay and wait to see Giulianella?

Federico. (*Rises.*) You're really going to go?

Rosa. Yes, Federico, he's really going to go! (Rocco *crosses to door.*)

Federico. I'd like to wait and speak to Giulianella, if that's all right. I would just like to give her my own point of view.

Rosa. That's all right, Federico, you can wait.

Rocco. Federi, I'll be seeing you.

Federico. (*He crosses to* Rocco.) Rocco. Won't you stay and speak to Giulianella too . . . please. (Virginia *starts cleaning Right end of table.*)

Rocco. Do you think I don't know my own mother? If I stay she will hit me with that plate!

Rosa. A good thing you realise that!

Rocco. I'll see you later. Ciao, Federi!

Federico. Ciao, Rocco! (*He hangs jacket on peg Right of door.* Rocco *goes out Up Left. A pause, then.*)

Rosa. (*She crosses Right, sits Left of table.*) And what has Giulianella been up to this time?

Federico. (*He comes Downstage.*) She wants to go on television.

Virginia. Television . . . (*She stops cleaning table, leans on table to listen.*)

Rosa. (*She cuts ham.*) That's my sister-in-law to blame! Aunt Meme runs everybody's life. Television! She knows someone who knows someone who knows someone who *might* give Giulianella an audition.

FEDERICO. Why can't Aunt Meme mind her own business? (VIRGINIA *crosses up to sink.*)

ROSA. Because, poor woman, since her husband died she has had no business of her own to mind. Besides, she thinks girls of today should work, do things, occupy themselves, and she is their best example. You've no idea of that woman's energy. She drove her poor husband to his grave, always treating him for this and that, diagnosing all his illnesses. If she hadn't told him that he was suffering from them, he might never have known. And now she brings up her son in the same way.

ANTONIO. Virgi—where's Virginia? (*He enters Up Left carrying a hat,* FEDERICO *goes Right above table.*)

VIRGINIA. Here!

ANTONIO. It's dark in here. (*Switches light on at Right of door.*) Put a shovelful of coal in the stove.

VIRGINIA. Signora? (ANTONIO *crosses to above table.*)

ROSA. Papa, I'm trying to finish tomorrow's ragu. If I have to have you under my feet, I shall never finish tonight.

ANTONIO. Five minutes, that's all. (*To* VIRGINIA.) Put a shovelful of coal in the stove.

VIRGINIA. Signora?

ROSA. Oh, put a shovelful of coal wherever he wants one. (*To* ANTONIO.) Is that Peppino's hat? (VIRGINIA *crosses Left below table to stove.*)

ANTONIO. (*Awkwardly.*) He asked me—himself. "Give it a stretch," he asked me. Besides, I like to sit a few minutes by the fire.

FEDERICO. Don Antonio, how are you? (VIRGINIA *gets two shovels from coal bucket. Gets hot coals from Upstage burner.*)

ANTONIO. Fine, fine! How are you? (*To* ROSA.) Who is he?

FEDERICO. It's me. Federico Sirretta.

ANTONIO. (*To* ROSA.) Has he come to fix the geyser

in the bathroom? (VIRGINIA *crosses Right below table with coals to Right stove.*)

ROSA. Papa, he's a friend of Rocco's!

ANTONIO. There's no need to shout at me, Rosa. These days you talk to me as if you had a lemon in your mouth.

ROSA. (*She rises, takes bowl of tomato puree and goes to stove, puts puree Down Center of Downstage burner.*) Because you refuse to understand a single word that's said to you!

ANTONIO. (*He crosses Right, puts hat on Right table. FEDERICO counters Left.*) Quite right, quite right! I agree with every word you say!

ROSA. (*She crosses to Up Left door.*) Virgi, I need you in the dining room.

ANTONIO. Where is the fan?

VIRGINIA. (*She crosses Left below table. Puts shovels back in coal bucket. Gives ANTONIO fan.*) Coming.

ROSA. You'll have to excuse me, Federico.

FEDERICO. Of course, Donna Rosa.

(ROSA *goes out Up Left.* VIRGINIA *crosses to the stove followed by* ANTONIO. *She gives him a straw fan and then exits Up Left.*)

ANTONIO. (*Aping* ROSA.) "You refuse to understand a single word that is said to you." That's the way she speaks to me. (*Tastes ragu sauce.*) They all do. They are waiting for me to go.

FEDERICO. That's a poor way to joke, Don Antonio.

ANTONIO. It's a good joke. Because the joke is on them. Because I am not going to die. (*He crosses to Up Left door.*) As long as I have my health and my hands and I know how to use them . . . Pass me that hat block.

FEDERICO. (*He looks at Right wall.*) Which one?

ANTONIO. There—the one on the right. Not that one —the one next to it.

FEDERICO. (*Bringing the hat block from the shelf to Center table.*) Here you are.

ANTONIO. Thank you. (*Handing* FEDERICO *the fan.*) Would you blow a little. (FEDERICO *fans the hat block.*) There— (*Points to Right stove.* FEDERICO *crosses Right to stove,* ANTONIO *crosses Right to work table carrying hat block. Puts it on stool, puts hat on block.*) gently . . . So . . . "You refuse to understand a single word that is said to you!" Is that the way to speak to a man who has worked all his life? (*Unveiling the table.*) This table could tell some stories! (*Pointing to the hat blocks on the shelf.*) And what about those? Eh? What could they tell you of the labours of Don Antonio Piscopo!

FEDERICO. (*He ties* ANTONIO'S *apron.*) Rocco says that you started out with nothing? Is it true?

ANTONIO. (*Fondly.*) Little Rocco takes after me. He's the only one in this family who knows what he wants.

FEDERICO. He's always talking about you.

ANTONIO. Because he's *like* me. He has his grandfather's head on his shoulders, has Rocco. A businessman's head. (*He picks up pan from bottom shelf of table and goes to sink.*) Listen, when Rocco opens his own shop in Via Calabritto, he'll surprise everybody. Like I did, when I first opened the shop in Rettifilo.

FEDERICO. Don Peppino's shop?

ANTONIO. (*Turns on water.*) The same. After ten years I had turned it into a store with two entrances with swing doors and four big glass windows. Across the four windows in curling gold letters it said: "Piscopo Antonio—Hat Maker." Peppino worked for me then before he married my Rosa. (*He turns off water, brings pan to table.*) He was my manager and then I made him a partner and we became "Piscopo and Priore Hatmakers & Gentlemen's Outfitters," because Peppino didn't think there was any future left in hats alone. (*Crosses to Right table. Pointing to shelf of hat blocks.*) And that's all that is left of the business I began in Banchi Nuovi sixty years ago. And this was the same table I had then and there stands the same iron.

FEDERICO. (*He breaks Downstage.*) And all this time you have kept them as souvenirs?

ANTONIO. (*He picks up hat block and hat and puts them on his table.*) I kept them because I still use them—a man should never forget how to use his tools. If I wanted, I could always go back to hats again. (*He stretches hat, then brushes hat.*) There are men left who remember me as the best hatter in Napoli. Do you know what they used to call me? The King of the Boater.

FEDERICO. The Boater?

ANTONIO. The straw boater. (*He crosses to table with block and hat.*) In 1920 I launched the famous Piscopo Boater. (*He stretches hat again, then puts wet cloth around it.*) In 1925 I launched on the market the celebrated rag cap, which could be folded when not in use and placed in the pocket like a handkerchief.

FEDERICO. (*He follows* ANTONIO.) You were a great inventor, Don Antonio!

ANTONIO. (*Shaking his head.*) I was a fool to myself. (*He crosses to Right table, gets iron from stove and iron stand from his table.*) Men began to go about with their hats in their pockets. After a while they began to realize that they could go out without any hats at all. (*He returns to Center table.*)

FEDERICO. And that became the fashion?

ANTONIO. (*Irons hat.*) Fashions can change. Listen, I can change the fashion. I have not been well lately—but I feel I am getting better all the time, and when I do—then I shall open another shop of my own.

FEDERICO. Really?

ANTONIO. I shall launch onto the market the Jackpot Hat.

FEDERICO. The Jackpot Hat? What does it do?

ANTONIO. It doesn't do anything. You put it on your head.

FEDERICO. What's new about that?

ANTONIO. The competition is new—with hats. Everything else in the shops today is competition: toothpaste, cornflakes, win this, win that. I'm introducing a competition with the Jackpot Hat.

FEDERICO. (*He crosses to Left of* ANTONIO.) What do you have to do? How do I win?

ROSA. (*Off.*) Virgi, be careful—you try to carry too many and you'll break them.

(ANTONIO *crosses Right with hat block and hat.*
FEDERICO *crosses Right, puts water pan on bottom
shelf and iron and iron stand on top of table.
Then he crosses to sink and leaves fan on Right
on sink.* FEDERICO *holds Up Left.*)

ANTONIO. I'll tell you another time—if I mention it in front of my daughter she says I am going crazy. (ROSA *enters Up Left, followed by* VIRGINIA *who is carrying a pile of plates.*)

ROSA. (*Indicating the sink.*) Put them over there. And then you can bring down the serving dishes, the ones that are laid on the dining table.

VIRGINIA. (*She crosses to sink, leaves plates there.*) Very well.

GIULIANELLA. (*She enters Up Left carrying a shopping bag, a magazine and wears a shoulder strap bag over her shoulder. She goes to* ROSA *and gives her a kiss.*) Buona sera, mamma.

(VIRGINIA *exits Up Left.* GIULIANELLA *crosses Right
to table, puts paper bag and magazine on Left
end of table.*)

GIULIANELLA. Buona sera, mama. (ROSA, *grunts, by way of reply.*) It took me hours to find the right colours for dyeing that material—I had to go round every shop. I spent all of the five thousand lire that

Papa gave me yesterday. (*Pushes* FEDERICO *out of her way as* GIULIANELLA *crosses and kisses her grandfather then crosses to Left of table, sits.* AUNT MEME *enters, accompanied by her son,* ATTILIO, AUNT MEME *is over sixty, but she carries her age well—in fact, she is inclined to ignore it.* ATTILIO *lives constantly under his mother's shadow—although he is thirty years old, he never ventures an opinion, or indeed a step, without first seeking his mother's advice. He stops a few paces from the door waiting for his mother to tell him what to do with the packages he is carrying.*)

MEME. Buona sera, Tutti. (*Goes above table to Right of table, she puts purse, gloves and umbrella on table.* ATTILIO *holds inside door. They ad-lib greetings back to her.*)

ROSA. What did the doctor have to say this time, Attilio?

MEME. (*Referring to her son.*) He's not running a temperature—but he's still having trouble with his bowels. (*She sits Right of table.*)

ATTILIO. (*Slowly—emphasizing every word.*) Yes, yes, I have to wrap up well. I have to keep warm.

MEME. What are you standing there for—put them down. (ATTILIO *looks around for somewhere to lay his parcels. Puts them on the floor.*) On the table. (ATTILIO *picks up bags and crosses Right to table and puts down the packages on the Right end of the table.* PEPPINO *enters Up Left, carrying the clock he took out with him.* MEME *takes off jacket and gives it to* ATTILIO.)

PEPPINO. It should keep perfect time, I've altered the regulator. (ATTILIO *takes bottles and cotton from bag.*) Donna Meme, would you do me a great personal favour? Please? When you go out of the house would you try to make sure that you take your own key— not mine? (PEPPINO *crosses Right below table.* ANTONIO *puts hat behind his back.*)

MEME. Don Peppino, you were the first one to leave this morning—if there was any wrong key-taking, it must have been you who took mine! (ROSA *puts tomato puree into pot.*)

PEPPINO. (*He hangs clock on Down Right wall.*) As always—twist everything round to suit your own argument! (ANTONIO *hangs hat on peg Right of door. Exits Up Left door wearing apron.*)

MEME. All right, if it makes you happy— I took *your* key. I didn't do it on purpose.

PEPPINO. (*Takes few steps Left.*) I'm not saying you did. All I'm asking is, in future, you examine the key closely before you pick it up.

MEME. Are you saying now that I've got bad eyesight?

ATTILIO. (*He goes Right to* PEPPINO.) Mamma darns my socks without having to put her glasses on. (ROSA *crosses Right to sink, gets fan, goes back to stove.*)

PEPPINO. What did the doctor tell you today?

ATTILIO. I have to take things easily— I'm suffering from— What am I suffering from, Mamma? (*He goes back to* MEME.)

MEME. Don't worry. Whatever it is, we're going to get rid of it. (*Examining the labels on the boxes and bottles, holding them at arms length in order to read them.*) A tablespoon of this after every meal; and these ones are to be swallowed every four hours through the day. (*She gives bottles to* ATTILIO *who puts them back in shopping bag. Everything is back in bag except cotton and vials.*) And these are your injections. Go to your room and get yourself ready. I'll be in as soon as I've boiled the water. (*She gives* ATTILIO *her purse.*)

ATTILIO. (*He picks up packages.*) The doctor said the injections might hurt a little.

MEME. Injections always hurt a little.

ATTILIO. (*Kisses* MEME *on cheek.*) Mama, try to be careful. (*He goes out Up Right with* MEME'S *jacket, gloves, purse and two shopping bags.*)

MEME. (*To* ROSA.) Where did I put my syringes?

(*She rises, takes vials, leaves cotton on table.* ROSA *indicates drawer Left of sink.* MEME *gets syringe box and white cloth, goes to Downstage end of stove.*)

PEPPINO. You'll see him off like you did your husband.

MEME. My husband suffered from arterio-sclerosis . . . in addition to diabetes. Not to mention prostates. Nobody knows what I went through. I had to force every teaspoon of medicine down his throat. I had to hold him down to give him his injections. In the last months he didn't even know what he was saying. He was in his second childhood. (ROSA *gets three soup bowls and four plates. Sets them on table.*)

PEPPINO. Donna Meme, you drove him to his second childhood.

MEME. (*She crosses Right below table for cotton.*) Giulianella, did you find the right colors? (*She crosses Left back to stove, she puts cotton rear of stove, she spreads white cloth Downstage end for needles.*)

ROSA. More expense that wasn't necessary.

GIULIANELLA. No, it isn't!

ROSA. You've bought twice as much dye as you need. You've never dyed material in all your life—it isn't easy—it takes practice.

GIULIANELLA. I'm going to practice with Mariolina. That's why I bought so much.

ROSA. Go on. It's your own time you're wasting. (*She gets silverware from Right table drawer and sets it.*)

GIULIANELLA. It's always the same in this house. Anyone who wants to do something worthwhile is time-wasting.

MEME. I agree with Giulianella.

ROSA. You're the one who put all these ideas into her head in the first place.

MEME. What's wrong with her wanting to *be* someone?

ROSA. She's engaged to Federico—shouldn't he have some say in the matter?

MEME. She's engaged to a blockhead. And I would say that to his face if he were standing in this room!

FEDERICO. (*He comes out of corner.*) I *am* standing in the room, Aunt Meme. (ROSA *crosses Left to stove, gets soup, returns to table.*)

MEME. You're a blockhead! Only a blockhead would hide himself away in a corner and not say a word.

FEDERICO. Grazie!

MEME. Giulianella's the only child in the house with an ounce of intelligence.

PEPPINO. Thank you. (ROSA *dips up soup.*)

FEDERICO. (*He comes Downstage.*) What about Rocco? He is opening a new shop in Via Calabritto. (PEPPINO *goes to Right of table, sits.*)

MEME. Rocco can open a hundred shops, wherever he likes. Rocco was born ignorant, like his father. (*She fills syringe from vial.*)

PEPPINO. Who's ignorant!

MEME. You know you are ignorant. You even spell 'intelligent' with two 'g's! (ROSA *gets glasses from drain board sink. Puts them on table.*)

PEPPINO. You don't need an university degree to sell shirts, socks and ties.

MEME. Life, Peppino, does not begin and end with the retail trade.

PEPPINO. What makes you think that you know so much anyway?

MEME. (*She stands above* GIULIANELLA.) I don't. But at least I read. Books, magazines. I try to keep up with the news. Giulianella wants a career— (*To* FEDERICO.) you ought to be proud of her. (*She returns to stove.* ROSA *gets bread and cheese from cupboard under sink.*)

FEDERICO. (*He crosses Left above table.*) Excuse me, but I was brought up to believe that it was the man's job to provide for his family. (ROSA *gets cheese grater from drawer Left of stove.*)

MEME. (*She crosses Right waving syringe, backs* FEDERICO *Right.*) "The man's job!" What you deserve is a wife who doesn't want to think. A wife who grabs the first man she sees and says to herself, "Thank heavens, I've found a blockhead for a husband who will provide for me." I am old enough to be your mother, but you and your ideas come from an age that was dead and buried when I was a girl. (*She grabs her coat from under* PEPPINO *on the Left chair and exits Up Right.* FEDERICO *follows* MEME *Up Right.*)

PEPPINO. (*To* FEDERICO.) You shouldn't argue with her; it only makes her worse. She knows it all and the rest of us are ignorant . . . with to 'g's. (*To* ROSA.) Where's the wine? (ROSA *points to the stove.* PEPPINO *rises and goes Left, above the table, to the stove.* FEDERICO *crosses Downstage, moves Right chair away from table.* ROSA *moves ham plate to the Right, she finishes cutting it into small pieces.*)

FEDERICO. Giulianella, you're going to listen to me . . . (GIULIANELLA *picks up magazine, holds it high so she can't see* FEDERICO.) and not that aunt of yours! This morning you walked off and left me standing in the street, just because I happened to say that I didn't like the idea of you going on TV. (PEPPINO *crosses to above table.*) Your brother's on my side; he agrees with me. Ask your parents—ask them if I'm right or wrong, ask them if you ought to listen to me. Giulianella, after we're married, we'll discuss everything together before we decide anything. (ROSA *tries to lower the magazine* GIULIANELLA *is holding.*) But the final decision must rest with me, as the man. Otherwise, what kind of a husband would I be? (*To the others.*) I'm right, aren't I?

PEPPINO. Do you mind? You're spitting in my soup. (FEDERICO *backs Right,* PEPPINO *sits,* FEDERICO *crosses Left above table.*)

FEDERICO. (*To* GIULIANELLA.) As it happens, the television business has solved itself. I've got a friend who works in the TV studios. I got him to look up the results of your test. You failed. (*Taking out a scrap of paper.*) Here's a copy. "Giulianella Priore. Unphotogenic. No perceptible talent." Read it yourself. (*He puts note on table, then backs Left.* GIULIA-NELLA *is shaken by the news but controls herself and replies with apparent calmness.* GIULIANELLA *puts her magazine on top of note.*)

GIULIANELLA. It was only a test. I failed. That's what tests are for—to find out whether or not one is suited to something. It's like getting engaged—that's a test to find out whether or not two people are suited to be married. (*She rises, crosses Right below table.*) Bad luck, Federico, because our test has failed. You're free to go wherever you want.

FEDERICO. You don't mean that, Giulianella!

GIULIANELLA. (*She crosses Left above table, puts dye samples and envelopes in bag.*) How long have you known me, Federico? Don't you know yet that I mean what I say? Mamma, I'm going to see Mario-lina to practise dyeing the material. (*Picks up magazine, purse and jacket.*)

ROSA. Do you have to do it now?

GIULIANELLA. (*She crosses Up to door.*) I'm also going up because this room stinks of onions and it's given me a migraine. Good evening. (*Opens door a little.*)

FEDERICO. (*He crosses Up to door.*) Look at me, Giulianella, before you go! These tears in my eyes are not just because of the onions! (GIULIANELLA *goes out. Opens door wider to exit and hits* FEDERICO's *nose. A pause.* FEDERICO *tries to pull himself together.*) Did you hear that? Arrivaderci!

ROSA. Federi, you're not going to go?

FEDERICO. A moment ago I felt like one of the family—now I feel like a total stranger.

Rosa. How do you think she feels? I know her. (*She clears* Giulianella's *plate, soup bowl and silverware to sink and also clears her own.*) She's walked out of the room and right away she's regretted her words. She's gone up to Mariolina's. Go up to her.

Federico. She doesn't change her mind that quickly, not Giulianella. (*To* Peppino.) Isn't that so, Cavaliere? (Rosa *takes* Peppino's *plate and soup bowl when he looks Right.*)

Peppino. Don't drag me into it. I don't want anything to do with Giulianella, or Aunt Meme.

(Federico *crosses Down Left, sits below stove.* Raffaele, Peppino's *brother, enters. He is carrying a Pulcinella costume.* Rosa *puts grater back in Right sink drawer.*)

Raffaele. Donna Rosa, I wonder, would you mind —just a quick runover with the iron? (*Putting the costume down on chair Left of table.*) I'll leave it here.

Rosa. (*She takes* Giulianella's *and her glasses to sink.*) Don Rafe, you and that Pulcinella costume! Whenever, you have a show on a Sunday I don't get a minute's peace from the Monday before—you pester my life. The red shirt, your tights, your costume has to be washed and ironed . . .

Raffaele. It isn't *every* Sunday.

Rosa. (*She crosses Left with soup pot and plate of chopped ham. Puts ham in pot.*) Thank God for that, or you'd wear my fingers to the bone!

Peppino. I don't know why you waste your time. (Rosa *takes empty ham plate to sink, returns to stove.*)

Raffaele. (*He crosses Right.*) Do you think I enjoy it? Do you think I wouldn't like to give it up—if only my colleagues at the dramatic society would let me? "Who else could do it?" They say. "Who do we have to play the part of Pulcinella?" "It's you the public come to see."

PEPPINO. Who?

RAFFAELE. Me! Who am I to argue? Do you want to hear what the critics said about me three months ago? I might have the clippings with me. Do you want to hear?

PEPPINO. No.

RAFFAELE. No?

PEPPINO. No!

RAFFAELE. No! A nice brother! (*He goes to door.*)

FEDERICO. (*He rises.*) I think it's time I was going too.

ROSA. No, Federi—you stay just a little while.

(LUIGI *and* ELENA IANIELLO *enter as* RAFFAELE *opens the door wider to leave.* LUIGI *carries a paper shopping bag.* VIRGINIA *follows them in and holds in door.*)

LUIGI. The great actor! The greatest Pulcinella in Napoli, everyone says so! (ROSA *wipes hands on her apron ad lib greetings.*)

RAFFAELE. No, no—the greatest in the world!

LUIGI. Buona sera!

ROSA. Buona sera, Don Luigi.

RAFFAELE. (*He brings* ELENA *Downstage.* LUIGI *crosses to* ROSA *after* RAFFAELE *and* ELENA *break Downstage.*) Signora Elena, you are even more beautiful today than you were yesterday—what will you be like tomorrow?

ELENA. You're always trying to flatter me!

LUIGI. (*He crosses Right above table offers his hand.*) Don Peppino—how are you?

PEPPINO. (*Coldly. Does not shake hands.*) Well. And you?

RAFFAELE. Signora Elena, would I lie to you?

ELENA. Yes!

RAFFAELE. (*He takes* ELENA *by the hand and seats her Left of table.*) Look at you now. You have the figure of a great actress, isn't it so? Look at us all!

Together we could form our own Neapolitan Theatre Company. Signora Elena, the starring role; Donna Rosa, the noble mother; Federico, the lover . . .

PEPPINO. (*He rises, takes wine bottle and his glass to sink.*) That's a good part for our accountant.

LUIGI. Yes, of course. (VIRGINIA *crosses to stove. Gets oil, takes it to sink.*)

RAFFAELE. And my brother, Peppino, he would play all the supporting roles. (*He gets his costumes from* ELENA'S *chair and puts them on Up Left chair.*)

LUIGI. We will see you tomorrow. Donna Rosa has invited us to Sunday ragu. (PEPPINO *returns to his chair and sits.*)

RAFFAELE. Then I wait impatiently for tomorrow. (*At the Up Left door.*) What?

PEPPINO. What?

RAFFAELE. What?

PEPPINO. What?

RAFFAELE. Did you speak?

PEPPINO. No.

RAFFAELE. Didn't someone ask about my rehearsal?

PEPPINO. No.

RAFFAELE. I thought you were asking about the work we were doing.

PEPPINO. No.

RAFFAELE. Do you want to know?

PEPPINO. No.

ROSA. (*Going to door.*) Buona sera. (*Pushing him out.*)

RAFFAELE. (*As he exits.*) Buona sera.

LUIGI. (*To* ROSA, *displaying a package he has brought with him.*) Now, try and guess what I have in here. (*To his wife.* ROSA *comes to* LUIGI'S *Left.*) And you keep out of it. No clues. Three tries.

ROSA. I have no idea.

LUIGI. Think! We were discussing Neapolitan dishes. And I mentioned this particular one. And then you said, "I'm very fond of those, but I haven't tasted them in years."

ROSA. We talked about so many things.

ELENA. Tell her, Luigi. This is how you are—aggravating! Why should Donna Rosa have to put up with you?

LUIGI. (*He turns to* PEPPINO.) Would you like to try? (VIRGINIA *dries silverware used for soup, puts them on area Left of sink.*)

PEPPINO. Why should I have to put up with you? Besides I'm going out.

LUIGI. When you hear what I've brought, you'll want to stay at home!

ELENA. Tell them, Luigi! It's some of the calamari that Donna Rosa likes so much.

ROSA. Not the ones that you do with capers and olives?

LUIGI. (*He takes packages out of bag as he speaks of them.*) The same. The ones that make your mouth water. I've brought the capers— (*Ad lib:* Ah.) and the olives— (*Ad lib:* Ah.) and the pine nuts. (*Ad lib:* Ah.) And I'm going to cook them, everybody else—keep away. (*Taking off his jacket. Puts it on Up Center chair and puts chair to the Left end of table.*) An apron, Donna Rosa.

ROSA. (*Handing him an apron from wall Left of sink.*) Let me *stand* near you, I want to watch.

VIRGINIA. She wants to see that you don't make a mess of it.

LUIGI. (*Without rancour.*) You be quiet. You can be the maid.

VIRGINIA. (*Brightly.*) I *am* the maid. (*She gets oil and plate of garlic.*)

LUIGI. Pass me the oil then and I need three cloves of garlic and a sprig of parsley. I brought my own pot with me. (*He produces the pot from his package.*)

ROSA. A special calamari pot as well?

LUIGI. Do you know how to cook calamari without

a proper calamari pot? We went to every shop in Napoli looking for the right one. (*Puts pot on table.*) And . . . (Virginia *brings sprig of parsley. He sniffs at his ingredients.*) Straight from the sea! (*Ad lib:* Oh! Oh!.) Like putting your nose in a rockpool. (*He crosses Right to* Peppino, *thrusting the package under* Peppino's *nose.*) Smell! (Rosa *picks up pot.*)

Peppino. They're fresh, I suppose.

Luigi. Fresh? They're alive! (*He crosses Left above table, he takes the earthenware pot from* Rosa *and displays it all round.*) I rinsed it in sea-water and then wiped it dry—my grandmother taught me everything I know! (*He picks up the oil bottle and is about to tip some into the pot when* Rosa *restrains him.*)

Rosa. (*She grabs pot.*) That's earthenware. You can't put earthenware straight from the shop onto the fire. (*Taking over.*) It needs to be rubbed with garlic first, or in three days it will crack straight through. What kind of a grandmother did you have?

Elena. (*To* Luigi.) Who is supposed to be teaching who?

Luigi. We are never too old to learn. (Virginia *crosses to stove.*)

Elena. (*She rises and moves Upstage.*) I think I can safely leave you to it. I shall be upstairs.

Luigi. (*He crosses Right and sits Right of table.*) I'll be up in ten minutes, no more. I'll just keep an eye on Donna Rosa first. (Rosa *puts package back in bag.*)

Elena. (*To* Rosa.) Are we going to mass together tomorrow?

Rosa. (*She goes to* Elena.) I'm going to early mass. There's no need for you to get up.

Elena. I want to see how you look in the turquoise cardigan.

Rosa. You're coming for dinner tomorrow, aren't you?

Luigi. Of course we're coming for dinner. (*He turns

to PEPPINO.) We've been looking forward to coming all week!

ROSA. Tomorrow, at dinner, I shall wear the cardigan.

LUIGI. I chose the cardigan, did she tell you?

ROSA. (*As if to say; what good taste.*) No!

ELENA. (*She crosses Right to* LUIGI.) I can trust him to shop for anything. He's got more patience than me. He not only buys the right things, he shops around until he finds the best price. (VIRGINIA *stirs ragu.*)

LUIGI. When it came to buying you a present, Donna Rosa, and she said, "I'd like to buy a cardigan for Donna Rosa." Ask her who remembered that you'd once said that turquoise was your favorite colour. Ask her.

PEPPINO. You.

LUIGI. Me.

PEPPINO. To talk to you is to make a record.

ROSA. (*She goes to sink.*) Because he's such a nice person? Because he remembers things about his friends? (ELENA *crosses Left, below table to Left of table.*)

LUIGI. (*He rises and goes Upstage.*) Not all my friends. But always to you, Donna Rosa. For you, I would throw myself in the flames because you are the perfect woman. (*He crosses Down to* PEPPINO.) If there is a person on this earth I envy, it is your husband . . .

ELENA. What what what . . . ?

LUIGI. Forgive me, my dear Elena. You too have many great qualities but Donna Rosa is the perfect wife. (*He goes Up Right.*)

PEPPINO. (*He goes Right, for his coat.*) Excuse me, I have to go out.

LUIGI. Are you going?

PEPPINO. I can't stand the stink of the calamari.

LUIGI. The fresh tang of the sea—you call that a stink?

PEPPINO. It's also very close in this room.

LUIGI. (*He crosses Down Right to* PEPPINO.) I was hoping to talk you into a few hands of cards—like last week. This week I'll give you four points start.

PEPPINO. My dear Accountant, you mean well, you are a nice, dear man—but there is a time for games and idle banter and this is not one of those moments. But you don't realize that. You don't realize when a man is in a mood for a joke and when he wants to be left alone.

ELENA. Forgive me, but you didn't ask to be left alone.

PEPPINO. Forgive me, Signora Elena, but I'm asking now.

ROSA. (*Embarrassed.*) Peppino!

ELENA. (*She crosses up to door.*) Then we'll go. And as for tomorrow, we'll see if your mood has changed.

ROSA. (*She crosses to* ELENA.) I'm sorry. (LUIGI *takes off apron, puts it on chair above table, puts on his jacket.*)

ELENA. Not at all. My husband always goes a little too far . . .

LUIGI. (*He crosses to* ROSA.) It's true! It is I who should apologize.

ROSA. No, no, no! He has so many worries—the shop —business worries, you know. (ELENA *opens door.*)

LUIGI. (*He crosses to above table.*) We were going anyway. The calamari can be safely left to Donna Rosa. (*He crosses to* ROSA, *gives her shopping bag. Goes back for calamari pot.* ROSA *puts bag down on floor Upstage of stove. To* ROSA.) A low flame, you understand? Over a gentle heat until they boil, and then left to simmer. (*He gives* ROSA *calamari pot.*)

ROSA. I'll see you out.

ELENA. No—no.

ROSA. Virgi, we'll see you tomorrow . . .

(VIRGINIA *shows the* IANNIELLOS *out:* ROSA *looks towards* PEPPINO, *but his back is still turned im-*

placably on her. A moment's pause, then ROSA
closes door.)

FEDERICO. (*Stands.*) I really think I ought to be
going too. What do you think, Donna Rosa?

ROSA. (*Out of patience.*) Federi, you must decide.
We have our own affairs to worry about!

FEDERICO. (*He crosses Up Left and gets his jacket.
Shaken by this brusque statement.*) I'll go.

ROSA. (*She takes white cloth,* MEME *Left on Downstage of stove to Left sink drawer.*) May the Madonna
go with you.

FEDERICO. I won't come for dinner tomorrow. I can't
eat at home either, because I've already told my
mother that I'm having dinner with you. I'll go somewhere else.

ROSA. (*She takes apron from chair above table and
hangs it up Left of sink.*) Do what you think is best.
(*She returns to table, gets oil, takes it to stove and
puts it on Downstage area.*)

FEDERICO. What do you think, Donna Rosa? Should
I stand in front of the church tomorrow? And see if
Giulianella speaks to me?

ROSA. A good idea. Go and stand with the other
beggars, asking for pity!

FEDERICO. Buona sera. (*He goes out.*)

PEPPINO. There was no need to speak to the boy like
that.

ROSA. (*She crosses to Center table.*) Listen to that!
All of a sudden the Cavaliere Priore has discovered he
has a kind heart. (*She takes garlic plate and parsley
to sink.*) After the way you behaved to the Ianniello's
a moment ago.

PEPPINO. The way I behaved! What about you,
carrying on like that in front of everybody.

ROSA. What do you mean, "carrying on like that?"

PEPPINO. You know.

Rosa. (*She picks up silverware—Left of sink.*) No, I don't know.

Peppino. Yes you do!

Rosa. No! No, I don't! So tell me! I only know that whatever I do in this house I am doing for nothing— for nobody! (*With rising hysteria, puts silverware in Right drawer, slams it.*) Do you know what *that* means, Don Peppino? I don't want to spend my life fighting—fighting with my children, fighting with the rest of my family— I don't want to have to do that any more! (*She crosses Left to stove.*)

Virginia. (*She leaves Up Left door open having returned to the kitchen earlier in this discussion, now intervenes.*) Donna Rosa . . .

Rosa. You shut up. You are not even family, to interfere! (*She crosses Right to above table.*)

Meme. (*She enters Up Right and crosses to table.*) What's happened?

Rosa. (*Slamming her open hand on the table.*) Here! Here! All my life here in this room doing everything for everybody—a slave! No thanks from anybody. (*She takes plates from table to sink.*)

Peppino. Nobody asked you to do it!

Rosa. Did you hear that? "Nobody asked you to do it!"

Meme. Donna Rosa, tell me what happened first?

Rosa. (*She puts plates back on table.*) What always happens? Me. Getting the meal ready for tomorrow. (*She crosses to stove.*)

Peppino. We just happened to upset the Ianniellos.

Rosa. (*She takes lid off ragu pot, puts it on loudly, throws spoon on stove.*) You can chop off my hands if I ever set foot in this kitchen again. My daughter cannot stand the stink of onions. My husband cannot bear the stink of calamari. (Rosa *takes off apron and throws it on Left chair.*) Well, if my kitchen is not good enough for them, why should it be good enough for me? If they cannot stand the stink of my kitchen, they should keep out. (*She leaves the kitchen by the Up Left door. From Offstage:*) My husband—in this house he doesn't exist! He goes to his shop, his so-called business—and ruins it. (*We hear a door slam Off Right.*)

PEPPINO. Do you hear that, Amelia? (*He crosses below table to Up Left door.*) Do you hear what a viper she's become? She's given up caring. I'm the last to count in this house. It's not just the kitchen, it's the whole apartment. (*He crosses Down Right below table.*) It's not like living in a home, it's like serving a prison sentence. I'm sorry, but I am not a convict. (*He crosses to Up Left door.*) I won't be here for Sunday dinner. I'm going to the country where I can breathe fresh and clean air. Don Peppino Priore is too well known, too respected to be ridiculed. I am not going to be made to look a fool in my own house! (*He takes his hat from a peg on the wall, Left of the sink, and puts it on. It falls down over his ears.*) This is not my hat! (*He takes it off and examines it.*) It is my hat! (*He puts it on again·and realizes what has happened.*) He should not be allowed to touch hats! Her father is ruining every hat I own! (*He puts hat on, moves toward the Up Left door.*)

MEME. (*She crosses to* PEPPINO.) Peppi, don't go.

PEPPINO. If I stay in tonight, Amelia, I will not be responsible for my actions. (*He goes out Up Left.*)

MEME. (*She comes to table. To* VIRGINIA.) What was all that about? (VIRGINIA *shrugs, gets cloth from sink and cleans the table with a dish cloth.*) Something's going on with the Ianniello's. You know, but you don't want to tell me.

VIRGINIA. No, Signore, I don't know.

MEME. No?

VIRGINIA. No.

MEME. No!

VIRGINIA. No.

MEME. (*Pushes* VIRGINIA *aside.*) Virgi, you can go.

(*Goes to the stove, opens Center stove drawer.*) And if nobody wants to cook tomorrow, I shall do it myself.

VIRGINIA. (*Takes off gloves, puts them on sink. Takes off towel tied around her dress and hangs it on pegs Right of the door.*) Buona notte, Signore.

MEME. Buona notte. (VIRGINIA *exits Up Left.*) God, what a household! They behave like illiterate peasants. (*She crosses to the light switch, Right of the Up Left door, and turns the light off.*) They don't think, they don't read . . . (*She exits Up Right.*)

ROSA. (*She enters Up Left. Subdued. She goes to the ragu on the stove and stirs it. She crosses to the cupboard under the sink and takes out a large white bowl. She puts it on the table. She returns to the sink, gets a tray of macaroni, brings it to the table and starts to break it into the bowl.*) Nobody asked me to do it . . . nobody asked me to do it . . .

CURTAIN

ACT TWO

*The dining room. A large oval dining table, laid for
twelve persons, takes up most of the room. Silver
cutlery shines on a spotless, tablecloth. A nine-
teenth century chandelier hangs down from the
Center of the ceiling, shining as brightly as the
sun which streams in through a wide balcony. The
Scene of gracious living would be perfectly set—
were it not for an old jacket and some wrapping
paper thrown across one corner of the table.
ANTONIO is trying on a new suit. He has a jacket
half-draped across his shoulders, and a sample of
the jacket material in his hand. CATIELLO, the
tailor, is sticking pins in the jacket and marking
suggested alterations with tailor's chalk.*

ANTONIO. If I say something is wrong with the suit,
you should listen to me!

CATIELLO. I came here on a Sunday, didn't I, to give
you a fitting?

ANTONIO. That has got nothing to do with it. (*He
picks up sample from arm of armchair.*) I am saying
that the sample of material I chose— (*Displaying it.*)
this one, does not match the cloth you have made up
into a suit! (*He points,* CATIELLO *takes sleeve from
table and puts it on* ANTONIO's *extended arm.*) All you
say is, that you came on a Sunday to give me a fitting.

CATIELLO. If it was Christmas or Easter, or any other
holiday, you know me, I would still come.

ANTONIO. And that has still got nothing to do with
it.

CATIELLO. (*He pins sleeve onto jacket.*) It proves
that I'm giving you what you want—my best atten-
tions. It's what you always get. You don't think that

41

if you chose a sample, I would make up a suit from a different material?

ANTONIO. You *have* done. Catie, here's the sample. Is this the jacket? Yes, it's the jacket. The same weight, the same cloth—but it's a different shade!

CATIELLO. You're imagining it.

ANTONIO. I don't imagine! I am not senile! I'll throw the jacket off the balcony! (*He crosses to balcony.*)

CATIELLO. Anto', did you leave the sample in your room, on the chest of drawers, beside the window—did you?

ANTONIO. I might have done.

CATIELLO. Ah . . . that's it! The sample has been faded by the sun, that's all. I would not *make* you a suit from a different material, Don Anto', you know me well enough to know that! I have made you a suit that is a masterpiece; I have made you a suit that makes *you* look like a work of art—is it likely that I would make it from the wrong material?

ANTONIO. (*He throws sample through Down Right door.*) I want the trousers wide at the bottoms, English style.

CATIELLO. You really want me to do that?

ANTONIO. Why not?

CATIELLO. You don't think it's a little . . . snob?

ANTONIO. I am the one who is going to wear it. (*He crosses to the open balcony door and examines himself.*)

CATIELLO. There is no need to look—the jacket will be perfect. I have stitched my heart into that jacket. I'll work on the final alterations, all the rest of the day, and you shall have the suit tomorrow—who can do more, Anto'? (ANTONIO *kisses* CATIELLO.)

(ROSA *carries plates and puts them on Right end of table.* VIRGINIA *carries paste bowls and puts them Up Right end of table. The two women busy themselves, finishing the laying of the table.* MICHELE *positions himself just inside the door, looking around suspiciously.*)

Rosa. Virgi, put those on the table, and then fetch the napkins. (Virginia *exits Up Right.* Rosa *spots a black wrapping cloth on the table.*) That's a fine place to leave a wrapping cloth! Doesn't anybody know it's bad luck to leave a black on a table? (Rosa *scoops up the offending wrapping cloth and tosses it across arm chair.*)

Antonio. (*He crosses Down Left.*) I'm having a fitting.

Rosa. (*She crosses Right above table.*) It's not a fitting room. Go to your own room. (*She sets glasses from Up Center of table for the Downstage settings.*)

Catiello. (*He straightens out black material.*) I wanted to go to his room, Donna Rosa. He has a full-length mirror in his wardrobe. But no, Don Antonio, must come in here.

Antonio. The balcony's through here. I want to keep an eye out for Rocco. (Virginia *returns with the napkins, she puts one at each place setting.*)

Catiello. Anyway, I've finished. A few minor alterations, all marked. Have a look, Signora Rosa. (Rosa *starts setting six plates Right of table.*)

Antonio. (*Downstage, plaintively.*) But I don't want to take it off until Rocco has seen it. He knows about fashion. "Trousers wide at the bottom," he said. "And the big lapels." I said, "At my age?" "Listen," Rocco told me, "In London the older the gentleman is the younger the suit is." (Catiello *takes jacket off* Antonio. Peppino *has entered Up Left. He has overheard* Antonio's *final sentences, but has not understood.*)

Peppino. What do they do in London? (*He crosses Right above table to Down Right arm chair.*)

Antonio. They mind their own business. (*Back to* Catiello.) And that's what I want, Catiello. And so don't go until Rocco returns. (*He picks up hat from* CATIELLO's *arm chair.*)

VIRGINIA. (*At Left end of table.*) It's no use waiting for Rocco, Don Anto'. He was rude to his mother yesterday.

ROSA. Again this morning he walked out of the house without saying a word.

ANTONIO. He's got a mind of his own.

ROSA. (*She sets six other plates, going Left.*) Whatever he's got, he's not allowed to sit down with us today.

ANTONIO. (*His hat in Right hand.* CATIELLO *tries to get it.*) But it's Sunday! (ANTONIO *puts hat in left hand.* CATIELLO *tries to get it.*)

ROSA. Sunday or Monday, it makes no difference. He does not come in here today.

ANTONIO. (*He holds hat in front of him.*) He came into my room this morning and he did not say anything. He didn't want to upset me. (*Gesture Right with hat.*) And he kissed me four times. (*Hat in right hand.*) Twice here and— (*Hat in left hand.*) twice here. That's two times more than usual. Because he knew he would not be eating with me today. (CATIELLO *tries to grab hat from* ANTONIO's *left hand.* ANTONIO *puts hat over his knee, tries to stretch hat and returns it to* CATIELLO.) Now I have no time, next time you come I give it a stretch. (ROSA *sets Up Left glasses.* VIRGINIA *exits Up Right after finishing napkins.*)

CATIELLO. (*Fearing for the safety of his hat.*) Thank you.

ROSA. (*Setting more silverware at Right end of table.*) Papa, it's time you realized: Rocco has no respect for anyone.

ANTONIO. Rocco respects me.

ROSA. He *pretends* to respect you—so that he can get what he wants from you. He came in and kissed you four times this morning? Good for Rocco! He didn't come in to see me, his mother. Not even to see **if I was alive or dead!**

ANTONIO. (*He crosses Right above table.*) Why should he come to see you? He comes into your kitchen and you throw him out. He doesn't come, therefore he is ingrate. I'll tell you what's wrong with you Rosa. Arrogance. You are arrogant.

PEPPINO. This is what your father thinks of you!

ANTONIO. (*He crosses Down Right to* PEPPINO.) As for you, Peppino, your fault is jealousy. You are jealous of Rocco. (VIRGINIA *enters Up Right with bread and puts it on Left end of table, puts pasta bowls on all plates.*)

PEPPINO. Jealous. A nice accusation to make to a father!

ANTONIO. Jealous. Because Rocco is cleverer than you, because he has more common sense in his little finger than you have in your entire upstairs. (*He goes Upstage.* ROSA *sets silverware and places glasses at each Downstage setting.*)

PEPPINO. Why should Rocco go into business on his own when the shop at Rettifilo can provide work enough for us both?

ANTONIO. (*He crosses Up Left Center.*) The shop at Rettifilo is old-fashioned.

PEPPINO. (*He rises and goes Upstage.*) Excuse me. The shop at Rettifilo was old fashioned twenty-six years ago, when you put me in charge and I told you that men cannot live by hats alone. (ROSA *sets silverware Left end of table,* VIRGINIA *exits Up Right.*)

ANTONIO. All right! Well now it's Rocco's turn. Let him have a chance to be his own boss, and not a shop assistant all his life. I gave him the money to open the shop, and if he needs more he can have more. The money is mine to give—remember that. I can send you all begging if I choose to, and if I do it, there'll be no regrets on my part. You hurt me and I'll hurt you. (*He crosses Right above* ROSA.)

PEPPINO. What do you mean—"hurt you?"

ANTONIO. Through Rocco. Whatever you do to Rocco you do to me. And you do it on purpose. All my life

I have worked. My shop was there before you. (*He rattles pasta bowl on plate.*) And if today you are sure of a plate of macaroni, you have me to thank for it. (*He crosses to plate.*) I warn you. Leave Rocco alone. (*He crosses Left below table.*) I'm going to my room.

ROSA. Good!

ANTONIO. If Rocco isn't sitting at that table at two o'clock, then neither is Don Antonio Piscopo. (*He marches out Down Left, triumphant.*)

PEPPINO. Does that sound like the voice of reason to you? (*He crosses Left.*)

CATIELLO. What about me? If the suit isn't ready on time, he won't pay for it. If it is ready and Rocco doesn't like it, he still won't pay. If I wait for Rocco's approval, it won't be ready on time. It's a vicious circle. You wouldn't have any idea where I might find Rocco. (*He is wrapping up the suit.* ROSA *sets glasses Right end of table.* VIRGINIA *enters with two decanters, puts one each end of table.*)

PEPPINO. Don't ask me. Ask Donna Rosa.

ROSA. Donna Rosa neither knows nor cares. Virgi, come into the kitchen. We've still got the salad to wash. (CATIELLO *picks up the suit and goes out Up Left.* MICHELE *enters Up Right carrying bowl of flowers.* VIRGINIA *picks up large tray.* ROSA *crosses to* MICHELE, *takes flowers from him and sets them Center of table.*) What are you doing in here? (*To* VIRGINIA.) Virgi?

VIRGINIA. (*To* MICHELE.) I told you to stay in the ironing room.

ROSA. I said you could bring him here, but not if he's going to follow me everywhere like a stray dog!

MICHELE. I could wash the dishes! (VIRGINIA *exits Up Right with big tray.*)

ROSA. (*Goes to* MICHELE.) You can't wash the dishes 'til we've dirtied them. I'll call you. (ROSA *bustles out Up Left above* MICHELE. MICHELE *follows* ROSA *Up Right.*)

PEPPINO. Are you Virginia's brother?

MICHELE. I am.

PEPPINO. And is this the way you dress when you go out to—er—meet people?

MICHELE. No, this is a beret I found in this house. Your sister said I could keep it. (*Pulls a cap from his back pocket.*) Here's my hat. (*He crosses Center.*)

PEPPINO. (*He crosses Down Center.*) May I see your head?

MICHELE. (*Returns cap to pocket.*) If you want. (*He takes off his beret, revealing a completely bald head.*)

PEPPINO. My God!

MICHELE. Laugh if you like. It's your home so I won't take offense.

PEPPINO. My dear Michele, there is nothing to laugh about. For me who knows your unhappiness, who knows your trouble, there is nothing to laugh about. Tell me . . . how do I say it . . . after you air your head in front of someone, do you feel better right away?

MICHELE. If I take off my cap and the man doesn't laugh, no, I don't feel better. (*Puts beret on.*) There's no resistance.

PEPPINO. But if it does come to a fight, do you lose *all* control?

MICHELE. The last one was taken into the hospital. Cerebal hemorrhage, three cracked ribs and a broken nose. He had a wife and three kids. When I heard about his family I was heart-broken— (*Off Left, we hear the door bell ringing.*) but at the time that it happened—

VIRGINIA. (*She enters from Up Right and rushes across the Stage above the table.*) The Ianniellos are here already. (*She goes out Up Left.*)

PEPPINO. Naturally the Ianniellos are the first to

arrive! (*A thought occurs to him and he smiles in anticipation.*) How do you feel at this moment?

PEPPINO. Do you feel like—letting off steam?

MICHELE. Like a boiler that's about to burst! I promised my sister I wouldn't cause trouble, but inside my head there's hammer beating. Boom . . . Boom . . . Don't ask me, signore!

PEPPINO. Whatever is inside you must come out. Don't hold it in because you're in my home. There's a man here, at this moment, and I wouldn't mind in the least if you exposed your head in front of him. To be honest, I'd appreciate it. (*He pushes* MICHELE *off Up Right.*) You go back in the ironing room and come in here with your cap down over your ears.

MICHELE. (*As he exits Up Right.*) It would do me good. Boom! Boom!

LUIGI. (*From Off Left.*) Happy Sunday to everyone. (*Off.*) Good morning! Thank you, Virginia!

VIRGINIA. (*Off Left.*) Shall I take that?

LUIGI. (*Off.*) No, no! I bought this for Donna Rosa, I have to put it in her own hand. (LUIGI *enters, carrying a carton of ice-cream:* Cassata alla Siciliana. *He is followed by* ELENA, AUNT MEME, VIRGINIA *and* ATTILIO.) Good morning, cavaliere!

PEPPINO. (*He and* LUIGI *meet Up Center.*) You sound very cheerful. (*They shake hands.* MEME *crosses to table, puts purse and fur stole on chair.*)

LUIGI. I am always happy on Sunday. Every Monday morning I start off the week looking forward to Sunday, I am happier as day follows day. (PEPPINO *crosses Left above* LUIGI *to* ELENA. LUIGI *counter cross.*)

ELENA. *You* seem in a better mood today.

PEPPINO. Yes, but I'll be even better tomorrow!

ELENA. Ah! Peppino and his moods.

LUIGI. Where's Donna Rosa?

PEPPINO. (*Suddenly petulant.*) In the kitchen, so please don't disturb her. (ELENA *goes Left to* ATTILIO.

ATTILIO *takes off his hat. Then, attempting to recover himself.*) She's cooking your *ragu.*

LUIGI. *My ragu?* I shall have to disturb her—but only for a moment. I want to see how the calamari have turned out. (*Then, displaying his carton.*) And I want to give her this! *Cassata alla Siciliana.* It's one of her favorites.

MEME. (*She takes off hat, crosses Right below table, pokes hat with hat pin.*) Is all that for Donna Rosa? Nothing for us?

LUIGI. (*He puts cassata table Down Center.*) Chosen especially for her—but I don't mind if she shares it with the rest of us. I remembered her saying that it was her special favorite.

PEPPINO. So today you rushed out and bought some.

LUIGI. Of course. Do *you* like *cassata?*

PEPPINO. I can take it or leave it.

LUIGI. Excuse me, I must just see if the calamari is ready. (*He exits to kitchen singing: La Donna È Mobile.*)

ATTILIO. Mama, is it all right for me to eat cassata?

MEME. All right, if you don't eat too much. Hang your jacket up in your room—you won't need it at the table. And while you're up there, I'll give you your injection.

ATTILIO. You've already given me my injection.

MEME. You haven't taken your pills yet.

ATTILIO. I don't take my pills until after I've eaten my pasta.

MEME. I know there's something I ought to do for you that I've forgotten to do.

PEPPINO. Amputate his head. (ELENA *laughs.*)

MEME. (*Unmoved.*) You can tell what day it is, my brother's in his usual Sunday mood. Very funny! Come along, Atti'. Excuse me, Signora Elena. (*She goes out Up Left carrying fur, hat and purse.*)

ATTILIO. You always tease my mother, Uncle Peppi, but my mother is very good as a doctor. She cured my poor papa until the last minute of his life. You wouldn't have known that you had a bad liver, if mama hadn't told you from your yellow eyes. Mama reads books, you know. She reads! (*With which,* AT-TILIO *goes out Up Left in search of his mother.*)

ELENA. (*She rises, crosses to Up Center of table.*) Poor boy— I wonder if Aunt Meme really knows what she is doing?

PEPPINO. He was almost a bright boy once. He could have helped in the shop. She never let him grow up.

ELENA. I know. She smothered him with love.

PEPPINO. Exactly.

ELENA. Don Peppino, you must not let my husband upset you. I know he goes too far at times—it's how he is. He's so passionate about friendship he becomes a bore. But there is nothing, nothing he wouldn't do for your family. He thinks . . . I've noticed this . . . he thinks you no longer like him. (ELENA *sits.*) What *has* he done? (PEPPINO *is about to speak—and then, changing his mind, holds his silence overwhelmed with a deep sadness.* ELENA *moves closer to him, in an attempt to come to a deeper understanding.*)

PEPPINO. (*Evasively.*) Nothing— I don't know— I'm in this mood—it is the weather—

ELENA. *Please,* if my husband has done anything at all to hurt you—then tell me what it is.

PEPPINO. What is there to tell, when you know already?

ELENA. I don't! Believe me, Don Peppino, I have not the slightest idea!

PEPPINO. Then give me your hand— (*She gives him hand.*) and we'll pretend it is not happening. (*He crosses Left above table.*)

ELENA. But I still don't know what you're talking about!

LUIGI. (*Off.*) What happened here?

VIRGINIA. (*Off Up Right.*) It must have been an accident.

LUIGI. (*Off.*) It was not an accident. (*He enters Up Right.*) It can't be an accident—it's been done deliberately!

ELENA. What has? (PEPPINO *crosses to Left end of table.*)

LUIGI. The calamari. I went to look in the pot—someone has filled it up to the brim with garbage!

ELENA. But that's ridiculous—

LUIGI. Garbage! You can see it floating—used matches, pieces of eggshell, coffee grounds, There's even a bit of a stamped addressed postcard. Go and see for yourself—the stamp's come unstuck!

ELENA. Nobody would do such a thing!

LUIGI. Somebody has! Cavaliere, who could have done it?

PEPPINO. I don't know what you're talking about, I haven't been near the kitchen.

LUIGI. Well it obviously wasn't you. It was you, wasn't it?

ELENA. Of course it wasn't. It must have been an accident!

LUIGI. What kind of an accident? Donna Rosa is most upset—perhaps you could go and talk to her.

(ELENA *goes out Up Right.* LUIGI *crosses onto the balcony.* PEPPINO *watches him closely.* LUIGI *looks up at the sun.* PEPPINO *crosses the room and goes out Up Right. He re-enters a moment later pushing* MICHELE. PEPPINO *indicates* LUIGI *on the balcony. He goes over and calls to him.*)

PEPPINO. Don Luigi, do you have a moment?

LUIGI. (*He enters from the balcony and comes face to face with* MICHELE *who has his cap well pulled down over his forehead. They stare at each other;* LUIGI *is at first puzzled but unimpressed. Then, slowly,* MICHELE *removes his cap—a well-practiced ritual.* LUIGI *is fascinated, then, without so much as a smile. As* MICHELE *takes off his cap,* PEPPINO *turns Right,*

LUIGI *claps his hands,* PEPPINO *turns Left expecting to see a wounded* LUIGI.) Marvelous! Magnificent! (*Turning to* PEPPINO.) Where did you find that?

PEPPINO. I didn't find "it" anywhere.

LUIGI. Well, who are you?

MICHELE. (*Flattered by* LUIGI's *admiration.*) My name is Michele. I'm Virginia's brother.

LUIGI. (*Extending his hand.*) Luigi Ianniello. I'm delighted— (*They shake hands,* MICHELE's *power forces* LUIGI *to his knees.*) to meet you. What a face! Like a— Well, like an Egyptian wall-carving, or a piece of rare ivory. No, No! A terra cotta from Pompei. (*To* PEPPINO.) Have you had him long?

PEPPINO. Aren't you going to laugh?

LUIGI. Laugh! I'm astounded—amazed—but laugh. Anything but laugh. (*Back to* MICHELE, LUIGI *leads* MICHELE *Down Left.*) Have you ever been photographed—professionally?

MICHELE. Never.

LUIGI. I wonder if you'd mind—posing for me? Of course, with me it's only a hobby—but you could do worse. Shall I come to you or will you come to me?

MICHELE. I'll come to you.

LUIGI. Good! My flat is right above this one. How about tomorrow morning? For every picture I take I'll give you a couple of prints—free.

MICHELE. You're very kind. (*He offers to shake hands.* LUIGI *withdraws his hand.*)

PEPPINO. (*He pushes* MICHELE *Right.*) Would you mind going back to the ironing room—and staying there!

LUIGI. Until tomorrow! (PEPPINO *tries to kick* MICHELE.)

MICHELE. I'll look forward to it! Boom! Boom!

PEPPINO. And don't come back. (MICHELE *goes out Up Right mumbling* "Boom! Boom!" *to himself.*) What a face! What strength in it! I would like Elena to see him.

(*Off Stage, we hear* AUNT MEME *greeting the latest arrivals.*)

MARIA. Buon giorno, Aunt Meme!
MEME. Maria, give me a kiss!

(ROBERTO *enters first and crosses Up Right to* PEPPINO, MARIA *next, with small package.* GIULIANELLA *next with magazine,* MEME *last. The three ladies talk Left of table.* MARIA *has back to audience.*)

MARIA. Buon giorno, papa!
PEPPINO. Buon giorno!
ROBERTO. How are you, papa!
PEPPINO. Roberto, my boy!
LUIGI. Signora Priore, my warmest greetings. And to you, Roberto. (*The women chatter among themselves.* LUIGI *notices a package that* ROBERTO *is carrying, exactly the same as the one that* LUIGI *brought himself.*) Am I right in thinking that you have brought a little something for dessert?
ROBERTO. It's mother's favorite, *Cassata alla siciliana.*
LUIGI. (*He picks up his cassata.*) I brought some too. But Donna Rosa will find her son's *cassata* much tastier than mine.
ROBERTO. No, no, no! You were here first. Besides, you're a guest of the family.
MARIA. Giulianella, don't *argue!* You behaved badly, at least admit it!
GIULIANELLA. (*She crosses to Down Left arm chair sits.*) Federico behaved badly! He had no right to be there, outside the church with that silly grin on his face.
MARIA. You didn't even give him the chance to open his mouth. You walked off and left him standing there. I thought he was going to burst into tears.

ROBERTO. He *did* burst into tears. I saw him.

MEME. Perhaps Giulianella did the right thing. She *should* make it up with Federico, but not yet for a day or two. (*She sits Left straight chair.*)

ROBERTO. Federico is my friend and he loves Giulianella. Leave them alone!

MARIA. I felt sorry for him. So alone, like a little puppy. I nearly burst into tears, never mind Federico. And everybody saw you. They all know that you're engaged. No wonder he feels hurt!

GIULIANELLA. What did he expect me to do? Throw myself at his feet in front of everybody?

MARIA. (*She picks up box, coat, gloves, hat and purse.*) You'll go too far with him, Giulianella. (*Kisses* PEPPINO *and gives him the gift.*) If you behave like this you'll lose him altogether and you won't find anyone to argue better than him. I want to say 'hello' to mama. Come on, Robe'. (*She goes out Up Right.*)

ROBERTO. Excuse me. (*He gets both cassatas and exits.* RAFFAELE *enters Up Left, talking to* ATTILIO.)

RAFFAELE. (*He crosses Center, above table.*) Come along with me. You'll enjoy it. After it's all over we'll come back together. (LUIGI *crosses Left, talks to* MEME.)

ATTILIO. Uncle Rafe', the last time you took me to see you in a play I forgot it was a play—it was all so real I was frightened.

RAFFAELE. By the other actors, not by me. If I am on the stage, your uncle, how can you be frightened?

ATTILIO. I'd like to see you do Pulcinella.

RAFFAELE. Now's your chance! I'm playing him today. (*He displays the mask he is carrying.*) Aunt Meme, I'm taking Attilio to the theatre, it's settled. (PEPPINO *crosses Down Right and puts box and gift tie on seat of chair.* RAFFAELE *calling off.*) Isn't it ready yet, Virgi?

VIRGINIA. (*Offstage.*) Yes—coming!

RAFFAELE. (*Calling.*) Make enough for Attilio too!

LUIGI. Do you always eat before you perform?

RAFFAELE. I *never* eat. Not heavy food. And certainly not when I'm playing Pulcinella. A plain omelette, some green salad and a little fruit, that's all.

LUIGI. You give up your Sunday dinner—for the sake of Art?

RAFFAELE. (*Modestly.*) It isn't *every* Sunday. (*Sits on Downstage chair.*)

LUIGI. Even so . . . And is this your mask?

RAFFAELE. (*Proudly, displaying it.*) You won't find a better one. I bought it from an old actor who was having a bad time. It is made in the cast of Antonio Petito himself!

LUIGI. What do you mean—the cast?

RAFFAELE. The cast! A wooden mould, from Antonio Petito's own face! In the old days, the *real* theatre was the Neapolitan theatre, with Pulcinella. Just to wear the Pulcinella costume was to be a household name. And every actor who played Pulcinella had a mask made to his own mould.

LUIGI. Like Antonio . . . ?

RAFFAELE. Petito. Yes.

LUIGI. And I always thought that Pulcinella masks were all the same.

RAFFAELE. What an idea! Each mask was individually famous— (*Pulls out chair to put foot on it.* PEPPINO *makes a warning noise so* RAFFAELE *straddles chair.*) the Antonio Petito mask was the most famous of all. Today they are collector's pieces—works of art. (*Holding up his mask.*) Look—a thousand expressions are put together in this one face. It weeps, laughs, scowls, begs, loves, hates . . .

LUIGI. (*Sits.*) Make it laugh. (RAFFAELE *rises, takes off hat, puts it on chair, puts the mask on and jerks his shoulders up and down.*) That was laughing?

RAFFAELE. (*Takes off mask.*) Yes.

LUIGI. It seemed to me as if you were crying.

RAFFAELE. Impossible! Are you questioning an Antonio Petito mask?

VIRGINIA. (*She enters Up Right with salad plate and omelette.*) This is for you, Signorino Attilio.

MARIA. (*Entering Up Right carrying* RAFFAELE'S *omelette.*) Here, Uncle Rafe, it's ready for you.

RAFFAELE. (*He crosses Up Right to table.*) Who could ask for better service? (*He and* ATTILIO *sit down and start to eat.*)

MEME. (*She realizes* ATTILIO *is about to eat.*) Are you mad? Are you trying to kill yourself? You must not touch omelettes. If someone pointed a gun at your head and said: "Eat this omelette!" You must not eat. Green salad as well! (*Takes salad and omelette from table.*)

PEPPINO. Let him eat! You won't be satisfied until he starves to death. (RAFFAELE *takes omelette from* MEME *and dumps it on his plate.*)

MEME. Mind your own business, Peppi. (*To* VIRGINIA.) He'll have a piece of Mozzarella, six white olives and a glass of water with the chill taken off. (VIRGINIA *exits Up Right with two plates.*)

ROBERTO. (*Entering Up Right with a small bowl of sauce.*) We'll be sitting down in just a moment. The sauce today is delicious. (MARIA *follows in.* ROBERTO *holds out a piece of bread to* LUIGI *inviting him to dip it in the sauce.*) Don Luigi, would you care to try?

LUIGI. (*Crosses Right above table to* RORERTO, *gets bread from table.*) I do this at home all the time. My wife gets furious. (RAFFAELE *rises and tastes sauce, sits down again.*)

ROBERTO. Mama always used to say, "You'll spoil your appetite and you won't eat later!"

LUIGI. Exactly what my wife says. (VIRGINIA *enters from Up Right with plate containing a piece of Mozzarella, six white olives and a glass of water.*)

VIRGINIA. (*Pushes* ROBERTO *and* LUIGI *aside to serve* ATTILIO.) Signorino Attilio's lunch is served!

ATTILIO. It's not funny! I'm on a special diet.

LUIGI. But where is Don Antonio?

MARIA. Yes, where is Grandpapa.

PEPPINO. If Rocco is not allowed to come, Papa says he won't join us at table.

VIRGINIA. Donna Rosa has given permission for Signoro Rocco to come. (*Bell rings.*) It must be the Doctor!

GIULIANELLA. Aunt Meme, the Doctor's here.

MEME. I heard.

LUIGI. (*To* RAFFAELE.) What play are you performing today?

RAFFAELE. A classic. "Pulcinella and the Queen of Sheba." We've been rehearsing for eleven months.

VIRGINIA. (*She enters Up Left.*) The doctor. (*She exits Up Right.*)

CEFERCOLA. (*He enters, carries three books.*) Signori, buon giorno.

MEME. Doctor Cefercola.

CEFERCOLA. Signora Amelia. I return the books I borrowed.

MEME. It's such a joy to lend them to you. You always remember to bring them back. (*She leans down to Left chair when putting books there.*)

CEFERCOLA. (*He gazes at* MEME's *rear.*) I have a deep respect for other people's belongings. (MARIA *and* GIULIANELLA *giggle.*) Especially books.

RAFFAELE. (*He rises, has finished his lunch.*) I must make a start or I'll be late. (GIULIANELLA *exits Down Right, leaves her jacket and re-enters.*)

LUIGI. Your performance starts early.

RAFFAELE. Not till five o'clock, but I have to change. You see, the place where we play—it wasn't built as a theatre. There is only one dressing room. The producer's mother lives there. So I put on my costume here and then call a cab. I wear an overcoat, of course. Excuse me. Excuse me, Dr. Cefercola. Come Attilio. (ATTILIO *carries all dirty dishes and silverware. The two exit Up Right.*)

PEPPINO. Every Sunday, the same. He has to run about with a stomach full of food.

MEME. I admire him.

PEPPINO. Naturally, you would.

MEME. He's doing what he wants to do.

VIRGINIA. (*Entering Up Right.*) Donna Rosa says will you please take your places. She won't be a moment. (*She resets china and silverware where RAFFAELE and ATTILIO were sitting. ROBERTO and ELENA come on from Up Right.*)

ROCCO. (*He enters Up Left and shakes hands with LUIGI.*) Buon giorno. How are you?

VIRGINIA. Don Antonio. Rocco's here.

ALL. Buon giorno. How are you?

ANTONIO. (*Enters Down Left.*) Where's Rocco?

ROCCO. (*He crosses Left to ANTONIO.*) I'm here grandpa.

ANTONIO. Rocco, my darling boy, come and sit next to me.

ROCCO. (*He crosses Right.*) I'm sorry, I can't sit with you.

ANTONIO. (*He follows ROCCO.*) Why not?

ROCCO. Giulianella, I have told Federico that I'll call him from the balcony if he can come up. Now come on!

GIULIANELLA. If Federico comes up I'm going!

ANTONIO. What? What?

ROCCO. (*He turns to ANTONIO.*) Grandpa, Federico is my best friend and I can't leave him out there in the street. Not after the way he's been treated already. (*To GIULIANELLA.*) A child at school would behave better than you! (*Back to ANTONIO.*) But don't you be upset, eh? You just sit down and eat your dinner like a big boy. Don't worry about me. In my position, you'd do the same thing yourself.

ANTONIO. Why can't Federico come up here?

ROCCO. (*Shouts.*) Because Giulianella has forbidden him to.

ANTONIO. Giulianella, if you don't want to see Federico, perhaps you will be kind enough to go?

GIULIANELLO. Thank you very much! It's *me* who has to go because if Rocco goes, you will go too. (ROBERTO *pulls her back Right and makes her sit Down.*)

ANTONIO. Exactly! Because the whole bad mood in this house is entirely your fault.

GIULIANELLA. *My* fault?!

ROCCO. Whether it is her fault or my fault it is no matter, I'll go. (*He starts Up Left.*) I'm not hungry anyway.

ANTONIO. No! Don't go! God damn the head of the donkey! You do things to me on purpose, all of you! You find out what it is that I like most of all and then you try to take it away from me. What do I ask of any of you on Sundays? Nothing. I ask to sit down at this table, with my grandson sitting by my side, and eat a plate of macaroni. A plate of macaroni, that's all I ever want on Sunday. Because Sunday means a lot to me. How many Sundays do I have to live? (*All laugh.*) Laugh. Make a joke about it. Perhaps, when I'm dead, you'll joke about me. "Poor Old grandad," eh? "Remember how angry he was that Sunday?" All laughing because I'm not here to answer back. I hope you laugh so much you fall over and crack your heads! And when you do—think back to this moment—for it may be me up in heaven pulling the carpet from underneath you. So—all of you—remember! (*He coughs, crosses Left to his chair.* ANTONIO *is close to tears.* PEPPINO *steps in to save the situation.*)

PEPPINO. Rocco. Go down and tell Federico to come up here. (GIULIANELLA *rises.*) Giulianella, stay where you are. We will sit down and eat as a family!

GIULIANELLA. (*Sits again.*) You can't force me to talk to him. I shall sit and I shall not say a word.

PEPPINO. Good! It might save an argument.

ROCCO. Sit here, grandpa. I'll be back in a second!

ANTONIO. No, I sit down only when you come back.

(Rocco *hurries out Up Left.* Rosa *enters, wearing her turquoise cardigan and covered in trinkets and baubles.*)

Rosa. Virginia—we are ready.

(Virginia *goes out. All men rise. They all, with the exception of* Peppino, *greet* Donna Rosa *with "Ooohs" and "Aahs" of admiration.* Rosa *sits beside* Luigi.)

Roberto. Mama, you look wonderful!

Maria. But so elegant! (Roberto *crosses Up Center, pulls chair out for* Rosa.)

Rosa. (*With false modesty.*) Why not? Because I've been in the kitchen, it does not mean that I have to come to the dining room in a dirty apron.

Luigi. Donna Rosa, even *in* the kitchen, in a dirty apron, you are always the perfect lady!

Rosa. Thank you. I only wanted to show off the cardigan to its best advantage. It was a present from Signor Ianniello—I mean, *Signora* Ianniello.

Luigi. But specially selected by Signor Ianniello!

Elena. Who wants to take all the credit.

Maria. But what good taste for a man. Mama, it makes you look years younger.

Rosa. (*Good humouredly.*) And what does that mean? That usually I look like an old woman.

Maria. No! (*She brings* Peppino *to table.*) I only meant that sometimes the right garment can make even a young person sometimes look younger. (Virginia *and* Michele *enter, staggering under a dish large enough to contain two kilos of macaroni.*)

Virginia. Dinner is served, everybody!

(*They take their places at table. And now we should see staged an exact recreation of a typical Neopolitan Sunday dinner, perfect in every detail and ele-*

*vated—as every Neapolitan Sunday dinner is—
to the level of a family ritual. Plates are passed
from hand to hand with the expertise of a jug-
gling act. The plates form an ever-growing pile in
front of* DONNA ROSA *who then handles the silver
ladles with practised careless ease, anticipating
the appetite and needs of every member of her
family and every one of her guests. No one dares
object to* DONNA ROSA'S *apportioning.* ELENA *is
the first to be served; one ladleful only.* ELENA
would like to ask for more, but dare not. AUNT
MEME *is next: She receives less than a ladleful,
but this is of her own choosing, for she prefers to
have the rest of her portion served up later for
supper.* DON PEPPINO *receives his plateful with
indifference, he has other things on his mind.* DON
ANTONIO *does not like to see an empty plate. He
watches the large bowl, scarcely taking his eyes
from it for an instant, with great respect. How-
ever, he does not take his place at the table. The
conversation over the above is as follows.)*

ROSA. Elena. (*She passes first bowl Right to* ELENA,
and second bowl Left to MEME, *etc.*)

ELENA. Thank you, Donna Rosa. Just one ladleful,
please. I wish I dare ask for more—it looks so good—
but if I have too much in front of me I can't face it.
(*Muttered agreement from the others.*)

MEME. Not quite as much for me. I shall have a
little warmed up again tonight, for supper.

ELENA. It can't taste as good as when it's freshly
made.

MEME. I prefer it warmed up, so that it is burnt
just a little. I like it burnt—not too much—just round
the edges. (*Murmured notes of surprise, some of dis-
agreement.*)

ROBERTO. Mama, it's hot. Can I take my jacket off?
Today's ragu is exceptional.

LUIGI. As I can testify from the meat sauce. I've had a preview.

ELENA. You have been tasting again—you'll spoil your appetite.

LUIGI. No danger of that!

ROSA. (*To* PEPPINO.) Bon appetito.

ALL. Bon appetito. (*A respectful silence, broken only by the occasional shifting of a chair, the tinkle of glasses, the sound of forks on plates. The silence is broken by* DONNA ROSA.)

ROSA. You don't think it needs . . .

ALL. (*Ad lib.*) No!

ROSA. Papa, will you please sit down? (*Her request is backed up by encouraging murmurs from the others.*)

ANTONIO. No! I'm waiting for Rocco.

ROCCO. (*He enters Up Left, accompanied by* FEDE-RICO *who carries flowers behind his back.*) I'm here, Grandpa.

FEDERICO. Buon giorno, everybody!

EVERYBODY. (*Ad lib with the exception of* GIULIA-NELLA.) Buon giorno! (ROSA *rises and puts pasta into two bowls.*)

ROCCO. Mama, first of all, a big kiss for you! (*He crosses to* ROSA, *embraces her warmly, kisses her, and rubs his cheek against hers.*) Mama, you feel good enough to eat!

ROSA. (*Refusing to succumb to his flattery.*) You feel as if you need a shave.

ROCCO. I'm a big boy now, mama! (*He turns to* FEDERICO *who is still by the door.*) Federi', come on and sit down.

FEDERICO. Yes—I was—er—just looking round to see . . .

ROSA. I've put you over there, Federi', next to Rocco. (Rocco *takes two bowls to below table.*)

FEDERICO. Thank you. (*He goes round the table Right until he arrives at* GIULIANELLA. *She does not*

even look at him, when he offers her the flowers.
ROBERTO *shakes hands with him as he leaves* GIULIA-
NELLA. *He goes to his place, turns Right to* ELENA,
*offers her the flowers. She accepts, puts them on her
lap. He sits.*)

ANTONIO. Rocco, sit down! I'm hungry.

ROCCO. Coming, grandpa. (*He sits between* FEDERICO
and ANTONIO.)

ANTONIO. Where's my macaroni?

VIRGINIA. (*She enters Up Right with* ANTONIO'S
plate, which has been kept warm for him.) Here. (*She
places the plate in front of* ANTONIO, *crosses to Left
of table.*)

ROSA. Virgi . . . the napkin.

ANTONIO. (VIRGINIA *puts napkin around his neck.*)
Buon appetito, tutti! (*With the exception of* PEPPINO,
they all tease ANTONIO, *with muttered exclamations,
and:*)

MEME. Papa, it's too late for "buon appetitos!"

CEFERCOLA. We're already on our second helpings!

ROBERTO. Some of us have practically finished!

ANTONIO. And I am just beginning. And if "buon
appetito" is too late for you, it's just in time for Little
Rocco and Federico and me!

ELENA. Well spoken, Don Antonio! Very good.

ANTONIO. (*He rises, pettishly.*) Oh thank you. You
think I speak well? Perhaps I'll learn a little poem and
recite it after dinner. (*This remark is greeted with
laughter and banter.*) Rocco, you won't be offended
if I ask you something?

ROCCO. (*He rises.*) Ask me.

ANTONIO. You know how I always like to eat my
dinner out on the balcony?

ROCCO. I do.

ANTONIO. I seem to be able to breathe better out
there. (VIRGINIA *takes* ANTONIO'S *macaroni to balcony
table.*)

ROCCO. I know, you told me. (*He and* ANTONIO *cross Right below table.*)

ANTONIO. I want to go out there now. You won't be offended? As long as I know you're in here, I can eat my macaroni and enjoy it. When I doze off, you'll come out and take me up to my room, like always?

ROCCO. Of course.

ANTONIO. Preggo mi scusino.

(*They ad lib their assent.* ANTONIO, *helped by* VIR-GINIA, *goes out onto the balcony. He sits in chair,* VIRGINIA *takes blanket from chair, wraps it around his knees. Moves table in front of him. Perched out in the open air,* ANTONIO *tucks into the macaroni, blissfully happy. Inside the dining room,* ROSA *gives* PEPPINO *a sharp glance,* ROCCO *returns to his chair.*)

ROSA. Peppino, you're not eating?

PEPPINO. I prefer it lukewarm. Besides I'm not hungry. I'll eat it later—cold.

LUIGI. You don't know what you're missing. Does he, doctor?

CEFERCOLA. It's magnificent. And I'm the one who tells his patients: "Keep off the rich foods. Stick to plain, simple, nutritious cooking." This sauce of Donna Rosa's makes me a hypocrite.

(FEDERICO *asks for second decanter, empties it, puts it in front of him.* RAFFAELE *and* ATTILIO *with* RAFFAELE'S *overcoat now return.* RAFFAELE, *wearing his Pulcinella costume, leaps in pirouetting in the classic style. He bows to the assembled company.* MICHELE *enters, holds Up Right.*)

RAFFAELE.
Pulcinella . . .
Your devoted and demented servant

Who is both cheered at and jeered at
Applauded and defrauded
Takes his leave of his inestimable and inaudible audi-
ence
With a tear on his cheek as large and long as a water-
melon.
(*Applause.*) The theatre calls! Only the scent of a
larger audience lures me away—an aroma greater than
that of Sunday ragu. (*He declaims.*)
Let off the fireworks.
Good health and appetite to each and everyone of you.
From Pulcinella.
(RAFFAELE *takes off his cap and mask, bows to the
applause, throws kisses to everybody and exits Up
Left followed by* ATTILIO. PEPPINO *does not enter into
the fun.* RAFFAELE *returns to continue, followed by*
ATTILIO.) If this good company . . . (ATTILIO *pulls
him off Up Left.* VIRGINIA *sees* MICHELE *standing Up
Right wildly applauding the show. She screams at him.
Both exit Up Right.*)

LUIGI. What a charming man he is!

MARIA. All he ever thinks about is acting.

ROBERTO. Both in the theatre and out.

MARIA. Giuliane', what's happening about *your*
career? Have you heard anything yet about that
screen test? (ROCCO *signals with his hand for her to
drop the subject.*) What's the matter? Have I said
something?

GIULIANELLA. The test was no good. (*Ad libs.*) My
face is ugly and I have no talent. (*Ad libs.*) Ask
Federico, he knows.

FEDERICO. (*A deep breath, summoning all this
courage, then rises.*) Giuliane', I did not wish to raise
the subject of our argument at the table, but since
you force me— (ROCCO *pulls* FEDERICO *down. Then,
stumbling.*) Giuliane'—*please*—I'm really sorry—believe me—

GIULIANELLA. (*Ad lib builds through speech. She*

rises and turns on FEDERICO.) If you had one ounce
of dignity inside yourself you could not have walked
into this room! How can you sit there, now, making
a fool of yourself in front of everybody?

ROBERTO. Giulianella, will you shut up!

GIULIANELLA. I stayed here when you came in for
the sake of my father and my grandfather. But not
any longer. Papa, if you'll excuse me, I'm going to my
room. And you can all talk about me, if you wish,
without having to worry about hurting my feelings.
(*Near to tears, she moves to leave.*)

ROSA. Giuliane'?

MEME. Sit down and don't behave like a baby!

GIULIANELLA. No! *I* shall decide who I choose to sit
with! And if I can't have Sunday dinner with my
family without having to sit with total strangers who
have bad manners— I don't want Sunday dinner . . .
(FEDERICO *retrieves and presents flowers to her. She
hits him on the head with them and exits Up Left.*)

FEDERICO. (*To* ROCCO.) Did you hear that?

ROCCO. She *likes* you really. Give her a couple of
days to think it over.

ROSA. She doesn't know what she does want. That's
always been her trouble.

FEDERICO. (*Rises.*) Donna Rosa, will you excuse me?

ROSA. All right, Federico. (FEDERICO *goes to Down
Left arm chair and sits. There is an embarrassed silence.* DON ANTONIO, *who has been stolidly chomping
his way through his macaroni, unaware of the drama
in the dining room, rings a bell that has been on the
small table.* ROCCO *rises, goes to balcony.* VIRGINIA
enters Up Right.)

VIRGINIA. What is it, Don Anto'?

ANTONIO. Please may I have a glass of water?

VIRGINIA. Coming! (*She goes out Up Right.* ROCCO
returns to his chair.)

MARIA. Aunt Meme, is it true that you've started
writing a novel?

MEME. Who told you that?

MARIA. (*To* ROCCO.) Am I allowed to say?

ROCCO. "Am I allowed to say?" Why not? It's true!

MEME. And who told you?

ROCCO. I saw you myself. Early in the morning, up on the roof.

ELENA. What were you doing on the roof, early in the morning?

ROCCO. I often take my breakfast up there on the terrace where it's quiet and cool. You can see Vesuvius, the bay, the boats and the bathrooms across the courtyards. (*Men laugh—ladies shocked.* VIRGINIA *enters Up Right with glass of water.*)

ELENA. What?

ROCCO. I inspect them one by one. All the ladies taking their baths. In Professor Scarochini's bathroom, one of his daughters, you should see the volcanoes she has.

ROSA. You rush your breakfast and strain your eyes gazing at girls in bathrooms!

ROCCO. I take my binoculars. (VIRGINIA *exits Up Right with empty decanters.*)

LUIGI. (*Puzzled.*) Is Donna Meme writing a novel in the professor's bathroom?

ROCCO. (*He goes to* LUIGI.) No! Up on the roof. I've seen her up there, often, scribbling away in a notebook. I asked Giulianella what she was writing and she told me—Aunt Meme is writing a novel.

LUIGI. Is it true?

MEME. Yes, it's true. It's the only place in this house where I can find any peace. The doctor's been helping me.

CEFERCOLA. Only in an advisory capacity. And I can say I'm enjoying every moment.

MEME. It's almost autobiographical. I've written into it the story of my own marriage. Some happy memories and some disappointments, some sacrifices. Isn't it the same for everybody?

ELENA. Did you have to sacrifice a lot in life?

MEME. You're married, aren't you? Why ask me? Or is your marriage so perfect that you have not got a single complaint?

ELENA. I lead a reasonably happy life; I never said my marriage was perfect.

LUIGI. Why not? What's wrong with it?

ELENA. Oh, you! You're a man! Marriage was invented for men. (VIRGINIA *enters with filled decanters, gives them to* ROCCO *then exits.* ROCCO *pours wine at Right.*)

MEME. Is that true, Don Luigi? Are you completely satisfied with married life? Tell the truth. Has there never been one moment when you've been tempted to stray?

LUIGI. If you demand the honest truth—of course there have been temptations.

ELENA. (*She rises.*) When? You never told me! (LUIGI *rises,* MARIA *rises to hold* LUIGI. ROBERTO *rises to hold* ELENA, ROCCO *crosses Left above table with decanter.*)

ROCCO. Aunt Meme, you have set two happy people at each other's throats. (*Everyone sits down.*)

MEME. I have asked them to be honest with each other. Why not? When I fell in love with the lawyer who lived on the second floor of this very building, I was honest with myself and I was honest with my husband. I said to my husband, "This is how is is; and there is nothing to be done. And if you wish it, we will live apart. Remember though, that there is the child to be considered first." My late husband, whatever else he was, was no fool. And so we continued to live together. But we found our emotional fulfillment apart.

LUIGI. Donna Meme, you really are . . . an exceptional woman!

MEME. You say exceptional but you mean outrageous.

LUIGI. Oh, I would never dare to say that!

MEME. Why? Because you don't know how to speak the truth. Everybody knows about my wicked past—

FEDERICO. Everybody knows?

MEME. And if you didn't know before you do now, Federico. Peppi has always known about it because all my life I have told him everything. And Rosa has known. And Roberto. You all knew. My life is an open book and if it isn't, I mean to make it one. I've got nothing to hide. (*She lights cigarette.*)

ELENA. Excuse me, I hope you're not suggesting that the rest of us *have* something to hide. Because I personally have got nothing to hide about *my* marriage.

MEME. (*She crosses Right above table.*) I was excluding present company. I'm not saying there is no such thing as a happy marriage. But for every one that's happy, there's another that isn't. That's why I try to open Giulianella's eyes for her.

FEDERICO. (*He rises.*) Excuse me.

MEME. Don't take offence, Federi'—in marriage when you make a mistake you don't make it alone, you make it for two people. Of course, finding my own happiness cost me a great deal. People talk, they say hurtful things. They try to chop you in little pieces, but I knew how to resist. We were honest, the lawyer and I. He never behaved as if he was stealing me from my husband, so my husband didn't go through the humiliation of being robbed of his own dignity. There was no hypocrisy, no falseness, no abuse of confidence between us. We faced all the facts. Shall I tell you what I'm going to call my book when it's finished?

EVERYBODY. (*With the exception of* PEPPINO.) Yes. What is it?

CEFERCOLA. Do you mind if I . . . ? I'd like to announce the title— I'm rather fond of it.

MEME. Of course not, Doctor. Please do.

CEFERCOLA. It is to be entitled: "Yes, but you need courage."

MEME. (*She rises.*) No, no. "Yes, but you *need* courage."

EVERYBODY. (*This time including* PEPPINO.) Bravo! Bravo! (MEME *sits.*)

PEPPINO. Aunt Meme, it's exactly right! You need courage! To be completely honest—to be honest with oneself! But I'm only an ignoramus who spells "intelligent" with two "g's." But I have eyes in my head. I understand more than people think. The small details, the shadows in the color . . . hypocrisy, falseness, the abuse of confidence . . . I see them. I can't write what I see. At least I can put my thoughts into words and face all the facts too. (*A slightly embarrassed pause after this outburst, then.*)

LUIGI. Cavaliere, at last you've opened your mouth! That's the first time you've had anything to say since we sat down. (VIRGINIA *enters Up Right.* ROSA *has been watching her husband carefully throughout the meal puzzled by his behavior. She does not understand his outburst and she is afraid of it. She attempts to brush it away.*)

ROSA. Yes. (*Then, in an attempt to change the conversation.*) Virgi' you may bring in the meat and fried potatoes and the salad.

VIRGINIA. Right away.

PEPPINO. (*Rising suddenly.*) Enjoy your food, everyone. (*And he moves away from the table.*)

MEME. What's the matter?

MARIA. Papa?

ROSA. (*She rises.*) Do you feel ill?

LUIGI. Cavaliere?

PEPPINO. What's wrong with you all? All I said was enjoy your food.

ELENA. Where are you going, Don Peppino?

PEPPINO. Nowhere. I've had enough to eat.

LUIGI. But you've hardly touched a mouthful, I've been watching you.

MARIA. There's as much on your plate now as there was when I passed it to you—

LUIGI. (*Trying to turn it into a joke.*) Cavaliere, honor us with your presence, I beg of you— Donna Rosa will be offended otherwise.

PEPPINO. It makes no difference to Donna Rosa whether I eat or whether I starve! She cares more for your appetite!

LUIGI. Me? Why me? Where do I come in?

PEPPINO. Oh, come on, Luigi Ianniello, you're always coming in. You're in more often than you're out!

ROSA. (*Screwing up her eyes, as though peering in the dark.*) What are you talking about?

ROBERTO. I think that Papa means you're ignoring him in favor of the guests—perhaps?

LUIGI. Donna Rosa is only trying to be a good hostess.

PEPPINO. (*Losing control.*) Please Signor Accountant, do not speak—patience is patience and mine is finished! (*Nobody has the faintest idea what he is talking about, they exchange uncomprehending glances.*)

ELENA. (*She rises.*) Cavaliere, if we've done something to upset you, we'll go. Come Luigi.

ROSA. Who has done what? What patience? What is he talking about? Does anybody know?

PEPPINO. I *know!*

ROSA. Then tell us! Let's all know!

PEPPINO. (*Boiling with anger.*) Donna Rosa, there are things that are best left unsaid! So that Samson does not perish with the Philistines!

ROSA. (*Confused.*) Who are these Philistines? What are you talking about Philistines? Why don't you speak clearly?

PEPPINO. (*Backing down, deciding that he has said too much already.*) We'll discuss it this evening, Rosi, here and now is neither the time nor place.

Rosa. (*Determined to clear the air.*) *Why* this evening? What's wrong with now?

Peppino. In front of our own children?

Rosa. (*Totally baffled, flinging her hands in front of her face.*) Madonna mia, in front of anybody's children! What does it matter? (*She sits.*)

Peppino. As far as your mother is concerned, I no longer exist. I am but a shadow on the wall. I go out in the morning and my wife—she ignores me. I come home in the evening I say Hello, she turns her face the other way. Once if I wanted a handkerchief it was put into my hand, my shirts, my socks were laid out for me. Now I have to search myself for everything and anything. Sometimes I have to go to the shop in the same shirt two days running. For four months this has been going on—she is my wife and she doesn't speak to me. If I want a simple answer to a simple question I have to ask three times—every day, every night—at night—nothing! For four months and I can go to the calendar and prove that length of time. Every thing I do is wrong, nothing I do is right. Tell me that I am wrong in what I say and if you won't admit to that, at least admit that there is not much left of our marriage for you or me.

Meme. I think you've exaggerated a little.

Cefercola. Every marriage goes through an occasional crisis. The husband has his little ways, the wife has hers. (*He looks to* Meme *for corroboration.* Rosa *has not taken her eyes from her husband's face.*)

Rosa. (*Still calm.*) No, there is more to this than "little ways." Peppino hasn't finished yet: let him finish saying what he has to say.

Peppino. You admit that there is more? And you admit that you knew that I *know?* (Rosa *shakes her head emphatically.*) This cross that I have to bear!

Rosa. Everybody has their own cross to bear. Believe me, Peppi', I have my own.

Peppino. (*Turning to* Meme.) All these years, Aunt

Meme, and I'm just beginning to understand you. To admire you. You were right you know, the decision you chose. You spoke the truth and you faced the truth. Here, we are living a lie! (*Back to* ROSA.) Look at her! My wife! Sitting there smelling of cologne, wearing the jewellery that I gave her—*my* engagement ring, my bracelet, the one that I gave her when Roberto was born. (*Then, to* IANNIELLO, *accusingly.*) And *his* turquoise cardigan at the same time! And I have to carry the pain here, in my heart! And go on living, in my own home, while she carried on with her filthy, sordid *affair!*

(*This sudden condemnation occasions a stunned silence from everybody.* DONNA ROSA *neither challenges nor objects to his accusation. In her chair she turns facing Up Left.* MARIA *goes over to comfort her mother,* ROCCO *closes the glass doors to the balcony, wisely screening off his grandfather. A long pause, then.*)

LUIGI. Cavaliere, do you realize what you are saying?

ELENA. This is something new, quite different. (*Rising, to* LUIGI.) I think we should go.

LUIGI. (*He rises.*) No, Elena! I have no intention of going. Without answering these accusations? These people have been our friends for many years. Until one moment ago, I thought that the cavaliere was also my friend. Now, I have become a cross he has to bear. I imagine he has carried this pain in his heart for a long time. I must say that I respect his family and wife as I respect my own. Cavaliere, if you want you can believe these words of mine which are sincere and come from the heart. If not, I can only apologize for the mistakes you are making, which I perhaps have caused. Elena, now we can go. (*He takes a few steps Upstage, turns back to audience.*)

ROSA. (*She rises.*) No! Why should you go? Stay
for me. Stay for my children. At least they know what
is true. (GIULIANELLA *enters Up Left and, without an
inkling of what is going on, is drawn into the argument.*) Giuliane', come here. Did you know your
mother is having an affair with the accountant? That
is what your father says. Maria Carolina, what about
you? Surely you knew? Little Rocco, you are the
clever one didn't you realize that your mother was
going to bed with the accountant behind your papa's
back? (*To* PEPPINO.) No! You're the one who should
go—if anyone should go. Not Don Luigi, who all his
life has been a good and loyal friend to you. Ask
your own children. I have nothing to be ashamed *of*,
but I *am* ashamed when I look at you! You have seen
nothing! Nothing! You see what is not there; and the
things that *are* there you don't want to see! Not the
way that your children have grown up, and nothing
that I have done in this house do you see! (*She is
now gesticulating wildly.*) These pieces of furniture
have seen my fingers worked to the bone! (*She moves
around the room, striking the furniture with her fist.*)
And I have polished these pieces not only with polish
but with my heart! (*Down on her knees.*) Why does
this floor shine—because it's been scrubbed and rubbed
with my life blood every day of my married life! (ROSA
is kneeling on the floor. MEME *rushes across to help
her to her feet.* ROBERTO *helps* ROSA *up.* ROSA *trembling
with anger.*) And do you know when it began? The
day that I met him? And do you know when he began
to ignore his children? On the very day that his first
child was born! That day! Through there, in that bedroom! "Is Roberto born? Here is a bracelet." (*Exag-
gerates the gesture with which* PEPPINO *bestowed the
gift.*) "Is Rocco born? Here—take this chain. It's made
of solid gold." (*Another exaggerated gesture.*) "And is
this Giulianella? Here is a brooch—real diamonds."
Such big diamonds! And beyond the jewellery?

Nothing. Behind the gifts? Love? No. Indifference.
Arrogance. Blindness. (ROSA *pauses, searching for
words to express true feelings—she fails and continues
despairingly.*) I never want to hear your voice or look
at your face again! Get away from me! (*She tugs at
her bracelet and throws it at* PEPPINO's *feet.*) Here—
here is Roberto! (*Next, the brooch.*) This is Rocco—
there! (*And finally, the diamond clasp.*) And here—
(*The clasp sticks, then finally comes away.*) here is
Giulianella! I don't need these to remind me that I
had your children. You are the one who needs remind-
ing! (*She sits, pulls off her engagement ring.*) And
there's your engagement ring! (*Throwing that at his
feet.*) Remember that night? When you asked me to
dinner at Torre del Greco and what you said to me
at the table? Roberto! Roberto! Come here! (*She rises
and embraces him.*)

ROBERTO. Mama!

ROSA. Roberto. It's a miracle! It's a miracle that we
are alive, you and I! I tell you, Roberto, it's a miracle!
Robe', help me! (ROSA's *eyes close. She faints,* ROBERTO
helps her sit again.)

ROBERTO. She's fainted—

GIULIANELLA. Doctor!

CEFERCOLA. (*Rises, goes to her.*) No need for alarm.
She'll be all right? (*They all watch with bated breath
as the* DOCTOR *gives* ROSA *a brief examination.*)

MEME. Shall we take her to her room?

CEFERCOLA. She must lie down. She needs rest. Have
you a syringe? (MARIA *exits first Down Right,* VIR-
GINIA *exits next,* ROBERTO *next carrying* ROSA's *legs.*
GIULIANELLA *next,* CEFERCOLA *last, carrying* ROSA's
shoulders.)

MEME. I'll fetch you one. (*She goes out Up Right.*
PEPPINO *has remained glued to his seat during his
wife's outburst. He now seems to become aware of the
seriousness of the situation and buries his head in his
hands, his elbows on his knees.* ROCCO, *who has re-*

mained stationed beside the balcony, now intervenes, timidly.)

Rocco..Papa . . . ? (*But* PEPPINO *does not respond.* ANTONIO *has remained completely unaware of the drama in the dining room. He has finished his pasta and has been slowly nodding off to sleep. He jerks away and peers through the closed French windows into the room. He raps on the glass.*)

ANTONIO. Rocco!

Rocco. (*Opening the windows.*) Yes, granddad?

ANTONIO. Help me to my room. It's getting chilly out here. (*He rises, stretches and goes out through the dining room, assisted by* Rocco.) When Catiello, the tailor, comes. He doesn't want me to have the big lapels, or the trousers wide at the bottoms.

Rocco. I'll talk to him.

ANTONIO. If he won't let me have them I don't want the suit.

Rocco. I'll tell him. (*He and* ANTONIO *go out Down Left.* ROBERTO *hurries in Down Right.*)

ROBERTO. Has anybody seen the newspaper?

LUIGI. (*Discovering one on balcony chair.*) Here's one.

ROBERTO. (*Taking the paper and searching through it.*) I have to find a pharmacist who is open today. (ROBERTO *stuffs a prescription in his pocket and hurries out, still studying the newspaper.* LUIGI *follows.* GIULIANELLA *enters, in tears.*)

ELENA. What does the doctor say? (FEDERICO *crosses Right.* GIULIANELLA *is about to throw herself into* FEDERICO'S *arms, when* ELENA *gets her first.* ELENA *embraces* GIULIANELLA.) All right, all right, everything will be all right, Giulianella, just you wait and see . . .

PEPPINO. Damn my life. Damn it all. Damn every part of my life.

CURTAIN

ACT THREE

The dining room. The table has been cleared and restored to its everyday size. The chairs are now arranged round the table. It is early morning and, in the grey still-dawning light, we are uncertain as to whether the mood of the household has changed. The brightly lit chandelier provides a warm contrast to the cold morning which filters in through the balcony windows. There is a book on the table. A knife marking the place where the reader was interrupted: A half empty cup of coffee stands near the book. We discover PEPPINO, sitting in the Down Left armchair. AUNT MEME enters Up Right, carrying a glass of orange juice. She pauses and sips at the cup of coffee. PEPPINO, without moving, calls across to his sister.

PEPPINO. What time is it?

MEME. (*Looks at her watch, then takes off her glasses.*) It's only half past six. Would you like me to squeeze you a glass of orange juice too?

PEPPINO. No thank you, Amelia.

MEME. (*Joking but tender.*) What's this? All of a sudden I've become Amelia. Aren't I Aunt Meme any longer?

VIRGINIA. (*Enters Up Right.*) Here's the orange juice.

MEME. Ssh! Take it to her then. (VIRGINIA *takes the orange juice and goes out Down Right.*)

PEPPINO. How's her temperature?

MEME. All right. Going down. It was almost 100 during the night. This morning, when she asked for the orange juice it was right down. Ninety-seven. Don't worry too much, Peppi. She will be all right.

PEPPINO. Has her voice come back? Last night she couldn't speak.

MEME. (*Smiling.*) She still can't—until she forgets she can't, and then she's back to normal. The doctor says it's psychosomatic.

PEPPINO. Madonna mia, what's that?

MEME. It's nothing to worry about. She'll be fine, Peppi'. Would you like a cup of coffee? (*She crosses to table and tray with coffee pot and cups.*)

PEPPINO. Not just now. What a night! I feel terrible this morning.

MEME. There's nothing wrong with you either. You got a lot out of your system yesterday that should never have been there. (*She touches* PEPPINO's *forehead.*) Why don't you go to bed?

PEPPINO. No—no. We must treat today like any other Monday.

MEME. (*She goes to table, sits.*) You can't just *forget* yesterday, Peppi'. You have to make things up with the Ianniellos and also—through there. (*She puts on her glasses and reads her book.*)

PEPPINO. Later. I'd rather not think about it. (*He goes onto balcony, sits.*)

(ANTONIO *enters, in slippers, an old coat worn over his long nightshirt, a night-cap pulled down over his ears. He follows his daily morning practice of turning the switch to light the chandelier—in doing so he plunges the room into semi-darkness. He is somewhat taken aback and, not noticing the others, he switches the light on again.*)

ANTONIO. Meme.

MEME. Buon giorno, Don Anto'. Why did you turn the light out?

ANTONIO. Because I wanted to put it on.

MEME. It was on.

ANTONIO. I know it was on. That's why I turned it out. Because I thought it was off. It should have been off. My God, it must have been on all night. Who left it on?

MEME. We all did. We had a late night.

ANTONIO. If you had a late night why did you get up so early?

MEME. We aren't up early. We're still up late. (*She reads book again.*)

ANTONIO. What's wrong with everybody? Roberto and his wife are asleep on the living room couch. Have they been there all night?

MEME. If that's how you found them.

ANTONIO. (*After trying to work things out in his mind.*) I'm always the first one up in this house. I'm not very late, am I? I stayed in a little because the sheets were warm and the room was cold. I *like* to be up first. The house is best when everybody's sleeping. I can wander round and touch things just for the sake of touching them, without anyone asking me why. "Do you want something?" Do you know why I like to wander round the house in the morning? Do you want to ask me "why?"

MEME. (*She is deep in her book and not listening.*) Why?

ANTONIO. I like to see the sun come up, that's why. Do you know why I like to see the sun rise? Because when I was young I preferred to stay in bed. I'm trying to catch up on my life. I've missed so many sunrises in my time. (*Going Up Center toward the balcony.*) I like to sit over there on the balcony in the morning and wait to see what kind of a day it's going . . . (*He discovers* PEPPINO *in the balcony chair.*) Why, Peppi . . .

PEPPINO. Buon giorno, pappa. (*He starts to rise.* ANTONIO *motions him to remain seated.*)

ANTONIO. No, no. Stay where you are. Did you get up early too?

PEPPINO. I'm sitting in your lookout seat.

ANTONIO. It's not important, this once. I'll find somewhere. (*Going toward the kitchen Up Right.*) Is there anybody in the kitchen? Aunt Meme? (MEME *is deep in her book.*) I'm going to have a look through the kitchen window. (ANTONIO *goes out Up Right.* GIULIANELLA *enters, Up Left, in a dressing gown carrying magazine, and crosses to* MEME. *She puts her arm around* MEME'S *neck.*)

MEME. Giuliane' . . . Why are you up so early? Well?

GIULIANELLA. (*She sits Left of* MEME.) I couldn't sleep.

MEME. Try not to take it too much to heart. It is always the children who have to suffer! It will take time, I know, but you must try to erase it from your mind.

GIULIANELLA. Aunt Meme, what are you saying? Forget about Mama and the Accountant? We will never forget it as long as we live, Rocco and I. We were rolling with laughter half the night!

MEME. What?

GIULIANELLA. Yes, Rocco came to my room after the doctor left and did a fantastic imitation of Papa's great dramatic tragic scene! I didn't know Papa did that. I nearly died!

PEPPINO. (*Offended.*) I'm glad someone was amused. And have you finished laughing now—at other people's grief?

GIULIANELLA. Only for the moment. (*Then, with a giggle.*) Uncle Raffaele was right, you know. What he said, about us being straight out of a Neapolitan comedy. I'm dying of hunger.

MEME. Well, there is the meat from yesterday's *ragu* that wasn't even brought to the table. Have a slice of that; when it is cold it is much more tasty. (VIRGINIA *enters Down Right, crosses the room with the empty orange juice glass.*) Virgi, would you take the meat out of the cupboard and bring it in here for Giulianella.

VIRGINIA. The meat?

MEME. Do as I say.

VIRGINIA. All right. (*She gives* GIULIANELLA *a glance, surprised at her odd tastes, then shrugs and goes out Up Right.*)

MEME. I might even manage a tiny slice myself, just to keep you company.

GIULIANELLA. How's mama this morning?

MEME. She's all right. There's nothing wrong with her—but don't say I said so.

ANTONIO. (*Returning from Up Right.*) God damn the head of a donkey! What's happening this morning? I can't even look out of the kitchen window. That girl keeps moving . . . moving about all the time.

MEME. You want us all to behave like statues?

ANTONIO. I want you all to stop *moving,* moving about, everywhere, all the time. (GIULIANELLA *crosses with cup, hugs and kisses her Grandfather.*) Giuliane', keep still!

GIULIANELLA. Grandpapa, you don't *own* this building before breakfast. You're looking very handsome this morning. I might eat *you* for breakfast.

ANTONIO. (*Grumpily.*) Don't shake my head! I don't like having my head shaken!

GIULIANELLA. Every evening you *ask* me to rub your head for you.

ANTONIO. That's a different thing. In the evening I have a head that's been working all day. In the morning, my head likes to take things easy. (*Peering across at* PEPPINO.) Are you still sitting there?

PEPPINO. (*Half-rising.*) You can have it. I was just leaving.

ANTONIO. (*Waving him back into his seat.*) Don't move. I don't want to sit down.

VIRGINIA. (*She enters Up Right, carrying the plate of cold ragu, plates, knives, forks and napkins. She puts them on the table.*) Are you ready?

ROBERTO. (*Enters Up Left, wearing pajama tops over undershirt and slacks, drowsy and shivering, carrying shirt, jacket and tie.*) Buon giorno.

MEME. Buon giorno.

VIRGINIA. I'll bring the bread. (*Exits Up Right.*)

ANTONIO. (*Who has been giving the matter some thought.*) I think I'll go and take a look out of the bathroom window.

ROBERTO. Rocco's in the bathroom. Virgi, some coffee.

VIRGINIA. (*Off.*) Coming.

ANTONIO. Is your wife still asleep in the sitting room?

ATTILIO. (*Entering Up Left.*) Buon giorno. (ANTONIO *escapes Right.* ROBERTO *exits Up Right with tray, pot and cup.*)

MEME. Why don't you go and take a look out of the window of your own room?

ANTONIO. I've been lying in my own room all night. I'm tired of my own room. I know every single flower on the wall paper by heart. And will you all stop asking me, "Why don't you do this? Why don't you do that?"

RAFFAELE. (*He enters Up Right.*) Buon giorno. (ROBERTO *re-enters with tray, six cups, saucers, larger pot of coffee.* ANTONIO *stopped by* RAFFAELE.)

ANTONIO. Has somebody been round tipping everybody out of bed this morning? I'll be up on the roof. It's the only place where there's any peace in this house. If Catiello the tailor calls . . .

EVERYBODY. We'll call you.

(RAFFAELE *sits Right end of table,* ATTILIO *sits Right of* MEME, GIULIANELLA *to Right of* ATTILIO. MEME *pours coffee.* ANTONIO *exits Down Left. On his way out, he switches off the lights.*)

MEME. Robe', try a slice of the cold meat.

ROBERTO. No, thank you, darling. I really can't. I've got to rush away. I want to go home, take a shower and put on a clean shirt and get down to the office.

It's Monday morning. For once I'm glad the weekend is over—it was completely ruined by Papa, with all that idiocy.

GIULIANELLA. (*Catching her Aunt's eye.*) Papa, would *you* like to try some cold meat?

ROBERTO. (*He takes the hint, realizes that his Father is in the room. He grimaces, then:*) Buon giorno, Papa! I didn't see you sitting there! (MARIA *wearing robe and carrying her dress enters Up Right. Kisses* ROBERTO *and goes to* MEME *and is surprised to discover* GIULIANELLA, MEME *and* RAFFAELE, *all tucking into cold* ragu. VIRGINIA *enters Up Right with bread.*)

MARIA. Buon giorno. Buon appetito!

MEME, GIULIANELLA and RAFFAELE. Thank you.

MARIA. How's mama this morning?

VIRGINIA. Much better. She has opened her eyes.

ROBERTO. (*To* MARIA.) We'd better go in and say "Hello" to her right away, or I'll be late for work.

MARIA. I'm ready when you are. (*She follows* ROBERTO, *exits Down Right.*)

RAFFAELE. Isn't it strange . . . ?

MARIA. What?

RAFFAELE. . . . how a certain taste, or even a smell, can suddenly bring to mind the name of a forgotten friend, or a season of the year, or the happy memory of a past event, or remind us of something we've forgotten to do. Food talks. Take ragu, for instance. I smell hot ragu and immediately it tells me: "Today is Sunday." I taste cold ragu and it screams out "Monday." Duty calls. The bank summons me yet again to enter its portals. (MARIA *exits Down Right.*)

ATTILIO. (*He rises.*) I'm going to Aunt Rosa's room. I want to keep her company a little.

RAFFAELE. (*He rises.*) I'll come to say hullo to her.

ATTILIO. Uncle Rafe, may I say something? Yesterday I didn't enjoy the play at all. (GIULIANELLA *helps to stack plates,* VIRGINIA *clears dirty dishes and exits Up Right.*)

RAFFAELE. Attilio you are a born critic—nothing pleases you. Go to the movies. Don't come to the theatre.

(RAFFAELE *and* ATTILIO *exit Down Right.* MEME *goes out Up Right.* PEPPINO *has been considering an earlier remark of* GIULIANELLA'S *and now takes the opportunity to take it up with her.*)

PEPPINO. So, according to you, this family is something out of the Commedia Neapolitana?

GIULIANELLA. (*Reading magazine.*) Papa, are you still thinking about that?

PEPPINO. Of course I'm still thinking about it. Listen, really, you people, you really are a bunch of monsters. Yesterday this house was turned upside down and today you can eat, you can laugh, you can go about your own business as if nothing had happened. Nothing. Don't read while I'm talking. As far as my children are concerned, Rocco does imitations of me and you kill yourself laughing. As a family we come straight out of the Commedia Neapolitana.

GIULIANELLA. I'm sorry Papa, but it's true. You and Mamma have been making fools of yourselves, hurting each other like this.

PEPPINO. What do you mean?

GIULIANELLA. Why are you not more honest, more open with each other and call bread "bread" and wine "wine?"

PEPPINO. Bread? "Bread?"

GIULIANELLA. It's because you don't speak, because you keep things inside yourselves that they grow out of all proportion. If you have a complaint about Mama, you don't tell her to her face, you tell someone else. And then I have to listen to Mama complaining about you. You say this quarrel between you and Mama, has been going on for the last four months; but do you know what started it? I'll tell you. Four months ago, you and Mama went to Roberto's and Maria Carolina's for a meal. Do you remember?

PEPPINO. How can I remember one particular meal I ate four months ago?

GIULIANELLA. I can tell you and I wasn't there. But I know because I heard it from Mama. You had macaroni alla siciliana, with sauce made from fresh tomatoes and egg plant.

PEPPINO. (*He takes coffee* GIULIANELLA *has poured.*) Of course! It was delicious, I really stuffed myself that night. I had two huge platefuls and then I went back for more. There was nothing to quarrel about that evening.

GIULIANELLA. That's what you think. All through the meal you never stopped saying that Maria Carolina was a wonderful cook; and how it was the best macaroni alla siciliana you ever ate; and how Maria Carolina ought to come round here one night and cook it for us all and you still say there was nothing to quarrel about that night?

PEPPINO. I don't know what you are talking about.

GIULIANELLA. (*Takes her coffee cup to table.*) Look, Papa, I spent the evening with Mama when she came back from Roberto's. I had to stay with her. She was in such a state that I didn't dare leave her alone.

PEPPINO. Why? What for?

GIULIANELLA. Because of the way you insulted her at Roberto's.

PEPPINO. (*He rises.*) That is not so.

GIULIANELLA. I tell you, I have never seen anyone cry the way she cried that evening.

PEPPINO. Because of me! Because of the macaroni alla siciliana?

GIULIANELLA. Yes, you should have heard her: "Now, after a whole life spent in the kitchen cooking for him, do I have to be taught how to make macaroni alla siciliana by my daughter-in-law? And he had to have two helpings just to humiliate me." Papa, you're always criticising what she cooks for you.

PEPPINO. Well she is my wife.

GIULIANELLA. She said that she could never feel the same towards you after the terrible thing you did to her in front of Roberto and Maria Carolina.

PEPPINO. You really mean it Giuliane'? Four months of misery for the sake of a plateful of macaroni alla siciliana . . . well, two platefuls. (*Moved.*) Giuliane' come here, a kiss for your papa. (*She crosses to* PEPPINO, *kisses and hugs him fondly.*) Can you imagine how I feel? Even before you told me all this for the shame I felt inside myself for the way I behaved yesterday?

GIULIANELLA. You won't tell Mama that I told you?

PEPPINO. I won't say anything at all.

ROCCO. (*He enters Up Left carrying suit coat.*) What's all this hugging and kissing so early in the morning? (*Puts coat on chair.*)

PEPPINO. Rocco, would you do something for me? Would you go into the kitchen and call up to Signor Ianniello from the window? Tell him I'd like to see him right away.

ROCCO. At this time of morning?

PEPPINO. Rocco, just do what I ask you to do. He'll be having his coffee.

ROCCO. If you say so. (*He goes to kitchen Up Right.*) How's mama?

GIULIANELLA. Much better. Can't you talk to him later?

PEPPINO. He'll be going to his office later. I would rather get it over with before he leaves.

GIULIANELLA. What about mama? When are you going to see her? I'll come with you, if you're afraid to go in alone.

PEPPINO. I would rather settle things with Don Luigi first.

ROCCO. (*Returning from Up Right.*) He'll be down shortly, papa. Giulianella, Federico's standing on the street corner. Shall I give him a message for you?

GIULIANELLA. Give me a couple of minutes to get

dressed and I'll come with you. Don't you dare tell him I am anxious to make it up with him.

Rocco. He's my best friend. I tell him everything.

GIULIANELLA. (*She hits him with magazine.*) You say one word, Rocco, and I'll kill you. (*She goes out Up Left.*)

PEPPINO. (*Studying his son carefully.*) So? We have an actor in the family?

Rocco. (*Not comprehending.*) Another one? Who?

PEPPINO. A mimic joins the troupe.

Rocco. Mimic? Who?

PEPPINO. Perhaps you would care to honor me with a private performance? I would very much like to see your imitation of me. Giulianella says you deserve an academy award.

Rocco. Giulianella told you about—? And she's the one who asks me to keep quiet to Federi'! (*Moving towards the door.*)

PEPPINO. Rocco! (Rocco *turns.*) Before you go. (*Rises, throws keys to* Rocco.) I want you to take charge of the shop this morning. I won't be coming in until later. And then, I thought we might go together, and have a look at your premises in Via Calabritto.

Rocco. (*Delighted.*) I'd be grateful for your advice, papa.

PEPPINO. You seem to be managing all right without anyone's advice. I would just like to have a look inside.

Rocco. I'd like that too, papa.

ANTONIO. (*Entering.*) The doctor's here. (MEME *enters Down Right goes Left below table, takes off her hair net, sticks it in her bosom.*) I saw him coming up the stairs as I was coming down from the roof.

CEFERCOLA. (*Entering.*) Buon giorno.

PEPPINO. Buon giorno.

Rocco. Buon giorno, doctor. (CEFERCOLA *carries doctor's bag and hat.* ANTONIO *follows him.*)

ANTONIO. I'll look after that—give it to me.

CEFERCOLA. (*Handing over the hat.*) Thank you.

ANTONIO. Excuse me. (*He heads for the kitchen Up Right and his hat blocks.*)

CEFERCOLA. (*He and* MEME, *back to audience.*) Is there any noticeable change this morning?

MEME. She can't move at all down her right side—until she forgets to remember that she can't move down her right side, and then she's fine!

ROBERTO. (*He enters, dressed, followed by* MARIA.) We have to go, papa. Ciao, Rocco.

ROCCO. Ciao.

ROBERTO. We'll see you all next Sunday, at our house.

PEPPINO. No, you come here again next Sunday.

ROBERTO. After yesterday? Papa, next Sunday you come to us? Please? (VIRGINIA *enters Up Right and goes off Up Left.*)

PEPPINO. How can Maria Carolina cook for the whole family?

MARIA. Really Papa, you are terrible, I cannot forgive you. All week we look forward to Sunday, then you ruin everything. (ROBERTO *pulls* MARIA *Left.*)

VIRGINIA. (*Entering Up Left.*) Signor Ianniello is here. (*Everyone freezes, then all look at* PEPPINO.)

PEPPINO. Ask him to come in.

VIRGINIA. (*She exits Up Left. Off.*) Come in, Signor. (LUIGI *and* VIRGINIA *enter Up Left, rather hesitantly. He is taken back to find so many of the* PRIORE *family confronting him.*)

LUIGI. Buon giorno . . .

ALL. Buon giorno . . .

LUIGI. (*He crosses Right a few steps.*) You wanted to see me, Cavaliere?

PEPPINO. If I might have a moment of your time. (ROCCO *puts on suit coat.* GIULIANELLA *enters Up Left, now dressed. She goes to* ROCCO *and the two of them attempt to exit.*) Giulianella! This concerns you.

CEFERCOLA. Oh, Peppino . . .

PEPPINO. I would like you all to listen to what I have to say. (*A deep breath, summoning his courage, then.*) Signor Ianniello is a gentleman and a good friend, and I am a prize fool. (*Ad lib.*) And anyone who disagrees with that is as big as fool as me.

LUIGI. Cavaliere . . .

PEPPINO. Wait. It isn't easy. I am speaking from my heart. No interruptions, please. (*Pause.*) I have insulted my wife, I have insulted you, I have insulted your wife, I have insulted the family name, Priore, therefore I have insulted myself—no, I have not insulted myself for I am not worth insulting. Luigi Ianniello— Old Friend, if you would like to hit me now, hard, in front of my children, you have my permission to do so. (*Ad lib.*)

MEME. Peppi', is all this necessary? You have made a fool of yourself and I think we are all agreed. So why make an issue of it?

LUIGI. Let's speak no more about it. My wife and I have been discussing it and she—*we've* come to the opinion that I am slightly to blame. Without intending it, my behaviour has been out of place. Cavaliere, let's forget the whole affair. (GIULIANELLA *embraces* PEPPINO, MARIA *embraces* LUIGI.)

ROBERTO. Spoken like a true friend.

PEPPINO. Am I not worth reproaching? Am I to be treated like an irresponsible child?

ROBERTO. You mustn't speak like that, Papa. The accountant has just told you that your outburst yesterday was very understandable from the human point of view.

PEPPINO. And nobody wants to laugh in my face? And tell me how stupid I am?

ROBERTO. Papa, enough! Do you want to shake his hand or not?

PEPPINO. Yes, I give you my hand with all my heart. (*They shake hands.*)

EVERYBODY. Bravo! Good, very good!

PEPPINO. But there's one more thing . . . (*Big ad lib.*)

ROBERTO. Papa, I'll have to be excused. I'm late already. Be good, papa. (*He embraces and kisses* PEPPINO.) Buon giorno, everybody! See you all next Sunday. Maria Carolina? (*And, after a chorus of "Buon giorno's" and "Goodbyes,"* ROBERTO *and* MARIA *go out Up Left.* ROCCO *and* GIULIANELLA *follow.*)

MEME. Doctor, I wish to talk to you. Peppino, you must excuse us too. (*She and* CEFERCOLA *exit Down Right.*)

CEFERCOLA. Excuse me. We'll be back soon.

LUIGI. Is this the meat from the ragu?

PEPPINO. Please, help yourself.

LUIGI. No thank you. Not that I don't like cold *ragu*—but I have already had breakfast. (*Another pause, then affectionately.*) Cavaliere, you really ruined that beautiful meal for us yesterday. That's what I can never forgive you for.

PEPPINO. Don Luigi, allow me to kiss you—on either cheek.

LUIGI. Please, Cavaliere, there's no need . . .

PEPPINO. There is. I have to kiss you first, to be able to say what I have to say. (LUIGI *allows* PEPPINO *to put his hands on his shoulders.* PEPPINO *stares into* LUIGI's *face, as if looking at it for the first time.* PEPPINO *kisses* LUIGI *on both cheeks.*) You are a good friend—and yesterday I was about to kill you.

LUIGI. Cavaliere, don't even joke about such things!

PEPPINO. It's not a joke. It's the truth. And you must let me speak and you must listen to me. Yesterday I wanted to kill you. It's the truth, Don Luigi. You know that I have a gun in my room? I wanted to get the gun and shoot you. And every time you moved, every time you laughed—I was thinking, soon he won't be able to move any more, won't be able to laugh any more, won't be able to make any more jokes. You didn't know. You were sitting here laughing and joking, and those could have been the last laughs and jokes of your life. Would you believe because of a stupid misunderstanding, a shadow, a fantasy, one man can end up in a cemetery and one in a prison? That's the way my mind was working. Don Luigi, did you ever think that I was that kind of man?

LUIGI. (*He wipes forehead with handkerchief. Out of his depth.*) Cavaliere, please, don't talk in this way. You're upsetting me. (*Looks at his watch.*) Besides, look at the time. I have a dozen appointments this morning—all over Napoli.

PEPPINO. And we'll spend next Sunday together. Come for Sunday *ragu.*

LUIGI. Don Peppino, let's think about it. For businessmen like us, I'm beginning to think that Sunday is not a good day.

PEPPINO. What do you mean?

LUIGI. Exactly what I say. Life's misfortunes and disasters always happen on Sunday. Perhaps it's all because we spend all week looking forward to Sunday; and when it does arrive, it's never as good as we hoped it was going to be. It's Monday today, and already we're planning next week-end.

PEPPINO. All right. (*A pause.*) Everything's forgotten?

LUIGI. I don't even know what you are talking about.

PEPPINO. I come with you as far as the door. We won't make any plans at all. Don't say anything to your wife. Next Sunday, I'll wait until the whole family is sitting at the table, and then I'll come and call to you. Ask you if you want to join us. Then if you haven't made any other arrangements— (LUIGI *exits Up Left,* PEPPINO *follows.*) you can come down for *ragu.* On the spur of the moment.

(ANTONIO *enters,* DOCTOR CEFERCOLA'S *hat balanced on the palm of his hand. He has, of course, been stretching it.* ANTONIO *puts hat on top of* CEFER-

COLA'S *coat arm of Down Left arm chair. He goes
out, happy to have been of service to the Doctor—
or so he believes.*)

CEFERCOLA. (*Offstage.*) Don't worry, Donna Rosa—
and I say it's quite safe. I take full responsibility.

MEME. (*Offstage.*) You see? If the doctor says
there's no need to worry, why should you?

CEFERCOLA. (*Offstage.*) You'll need to take things
easy for a day or so, but there's no need to stay in
your room. (ROSA *enters, supported by the* DOCTOR
and MEME, *and closely attended by* RAFFAELE *and*
ATTILIO. ROSA'S *hair has been neatly combed, she is
wearing a housecoat and slippers and looks every inch
the complete invalid—which is what she wishes to be.*
VIRGINIA *is last one on with tray of water and glass,
puts tray Right end of table.*)

ROSA. But I haven't got any strength in my legs,
doctor. And there are so many things to do in the
house. Madonna mia! Who's going to take care of
everything? I can't leave it to the girl.

MEME. You just tell me what wants doing, and I'll
see that it gets done.

CEFERCOLA. (*Opens his bag.*) All you have to do
is to sit down and give the orders.

ROSA. What about my voice? What if my voice goes
again? You don't understand what I'm going through.

CEFERCOLA. What *are* you going through?

ROSA. I can't describe it. Like a bad dream, when
you can see your arms and legs moving and they don't
belong to you. (VIRGINIA *gathers meat, plates, and
bread together.*)

CEFERCOLA. A couple of days and you'll be as good
as you ever were.

ROSA. Doctor, I don't want to contradict you. You
know more about these things than me. But I know
what I'm suffering. Something has gone very wrong in

my life. Donna Rosa Priore will never again be the woman she was.

MEME. If the Doctor says so—it *is* so.

RAFFAELE. Donna Rosa, you have as many lives as a cat.

ATTILIO. Mama says that there is nothing wrong with you. (MEME *and* RAFFAELE *hit* ATTILIO.)

ROSA. Your mother only says that because she loves me— She can't bear to think of me being ill. But I know I am. (*She lifts her right arm with her left hand. When she lets go, her arm falls to her lap.*) Aunt Meme, Donna Rosa is not going to be with you much longer. (VIRGINIA *exits with bread and meat.*)

MEME. Rosa! Will you please stop talking like that!

ROSA. No, I tell you, it's finished, I've not long for this world.

CEFERCOLA. (*Indicating the easy chair by the balcony.*) In the meantime, sit in the armchair over there, you'll be more comfortable. Rest yourself.

ROSA. Thank you, Doctor. (*She allows herself to be helped into the chair.*) Gently . . . Gently . . . God bless you. You are very kind. (ATTILIO *puts blanket over* ROSA's *legs.*)

CEFERCOLA. Now, all you have to do is call your maid in . . . (VIRGINIA *enters Up Right goes to table for coffee tray.*) There she is! And give her your orders. She'll do what there is to be done. (ATTILIO *on knees Right of* ROSA.)

ROSA. Doctor, I don't think I have the strength. (VIRGINIA *picks up tray.*) Ame', you'll have to help me. (VIRGINIA *drops silverware as she exits Up Right.* MEME *picks up after her and exits Up Right.*)

RAFFAELE. I must be getting ready. It is almost time I was leaving for the bank.

CEFERCOLA. I thought the bank didn't open till ten. (MEME *re-enters.*)

RAFFAELE. I walk all the way, there and back, twenty-five minutes each way. I have to keep fit.

Donna Rosa, try to keep your spirits up. I will be home this evening.

ROSA. The Madonna go with you.

ATTILIO. Uncle Rafe', can I come with you for the walk? It might do me good.

RAFFAELE. Of course!

MEME. Rafe', listen to me! Under no circumstances is he to be allowed sweets!

RAFFAELE. Don't worry . . . I'll buy you ice cream! (*He and* ATTILIO *go out Up Left.*)

CEFERCOLA. (*To* ROSA.) Have you spoken to your husband since—yet? Have you managed to forgive him for what happened?

ROSA. Why should he need my forgiveness?

CEFERCOLA. For your own sake, Donna Rosa, if you cleared things up between you, you might feel better yourself.

ROSA. I don't see that it's important any more. I forget easily. That's the one good thing about my character, I don't bear grudges. (PEPPINO *enters Up Left and hovers by the door, unnoticed by* ROSA.) I am only sorry for him that he said what he did in front of the children. What a fool he made of himself.

CEFERCOLA. (*He kisses* ROSA'S *hand and goes Left.*) You'll have to excuse me, Donna Rosa. I have other patients to attend to. I'll call in again this afternoon to have a look at you. (*Quietly, as he goes out.*) Buona giornata, Cavaliere. (*Off.*) My God! What happened to my hat!

(MEME *looks at* PEPPINO *then exits Up Right.* PEP-
        PINO *moves into the room and stands looking at
        his wife. After some moments, she becomes aware
        of his presence.*)

PEPPINO. How are you feeling?

ROSA. A little better, perhaps.

PEPPINO. Well enough to talk to me?

ROSA. Perhaps.

PEPPINO. I would like to talk to you.

ROSA. Talk away. I am here. I am listening. But mind what you say. I'm very weak. The doctor says that I mustn't have any more upsets. (*She is unable to continue.*) I . . . I . . . it's happening again! The house is going round! The room is going round in front of my eyes!

PEPPINO. Rosi, shall I call back the doctor?

ROSA. No . . . No . . . (*In a weak voice.*) Meme, help me! Help me!

PEPPINO. (*He comes Right, pours water, takes glass to her.*) I am here. There is no need for Meme.

ROSA. No, it's gone again. When it happens I don't know where I am. What did you want to talk about?

PEPPINO. No, later. When you're feeling better, perhaps.

ROSA. Yes. Later. You have to go to the shop now. You'll be late. And we'll talk this evening.

PEPPINO. (*He paces.*) And we'll say the same useless things we say every night. The two of us, you and I, we have been together all these years, we have three children—and there is still not that complete honesty between us that we can say bread is bread and wine is wine. Yes, we'll *talk*. We'll talk about the weather and about the little things that are wrong with us. We talk about the dreams we have both had in the night. But the real things, the serious things—perhaps the funny things that come to our minds because of a simple misunderstanding between each other—those things we keep inside ourselves. And we keep them inside ourselves for so long that they poison our stomachs!

ROSA. Do we have to do that now? This evening we'll talk.

PEPPINO. No, Rosi', now. I cannot wait. There is something stuck in my throat, Rosi'. There is a snake in my throat and I must get it out. So that I can

breathe again. And feel well again. Yesterday I behaved like a total idiot. And if I say I am sorry to the
accountant in front of everybody, it's not enough. I
am still humiliated.

Rosa. But how could you believe such a thing? How
could you make such a scene as you made yesterday?

Peppino. Jealousy, Rosi. Jealousy. Blind jealousy
that brought all the blood to my head and kept me
from sleeping. You have heard people say that they
felt as if there was a bandage tight over their eyes?
It's true. It happened to me. Even my customers were
suffering. There were certain times, every man that
came into the shop became an accountant. I was talking to myself in the street. "Why this idiot?" I asked
myself. "Why? Who gave him permission to be so
kind to Rosi'? He doesn't miss a chance to make me
feel small. My wife can't finish a sentence or state her
smallest wish but he jumps to make that wish come
true." "Oh, I do like May roses!" You said that once
—once, in a silly conversation in the middle of
February. And that man, three months later—how
can he do it—how does he three months later remember it? He does. And he comes here, to this house,
with a beautiful bunch of the first early roses, for you.
He remembers Easter eggs, he remembers that you like
almond cake. I come home from the shop and you
show me a big package and inside it is an almond cake.
"What a kind man the accountant is—he remembered
me saying I liked almond cake." I had remembered
too, Rosi'. But I took the package with my almond
cake inside that I had bought for you and I put it at
the back of the wardrobe. It's still there. And then I
thought, why does my wife keep asking for all these
things when that man's around? And I told myself
it was because you wanted him to bring you things.
When he tells a stupid story, you kill yourself laughing. And if I tell the same story, nine times out of ten,
you say "I don't understand" or "I heard it before."

And if we are going to talk to each other with that complete honesty I mentioned earlier, then I have to tell you every little thing. Rosi', I have reached the point that at certain moments . . . Do you remember the little closet at the back of the shop? The one where I keep the vacuum and the polish and the cleaning rags? Rosi', I locked myself in that closet and I cried like a child. And I was so angry with myself that I hit myself hard across the face. And I had to wash my face, wash my eyes, so that people who work for me would not begin to understand. (*He sits Left of table.*) Rosi', I wouldn't wish such terrible jealousy on my worst enemy!

ROSA. (*She has listened to* PEPPINO *closely and has come to understand his torment. Now, she feels a sudden tenderness for him. Rises.*) It's not possible, such terrible jealousy for me. Peppi! How could you imagine, after all these years, at my age, with three grown up children, that the accountant or anyone else would look at me in that way.

PEPPINO. I was wrong about Luigi Ianniello. All right. But what about you? What about these last four months? When did you last put out a clean shirt for me? Never mind a clean shirt, only a pair of socks? Even a handkerchief? Something is wrong, Rosi'. Before, when I used to leave for the shop in the morning, I'd look up from the street and you'd wave from the balcony. For four months now you haven't been there —not one morning—and I'm asking you to tell me why you've given up the habit. Come on, tell me. Have the courage. It'll do you good.

ROSA. What courage? When I used to do it regularly you never even noticed.

PEPPINO. You've changed, Rosi. You used to like to do things for me.

ROSA. And if I've changed, you've changed too. Perhaps neither of us have been perfect recently—but to do what you did! To think that I was really having an

affair with Luigi Ianniello! Peppi'! Peppi'. Come here.
Sit down. Here. You've always been crazy, but how
could you ever have believed it for a second?

PEPPINO. I was jealous.

ROSA. There has never been any man but you—even
before you met me—and if as a girl I was not like
that, why should I be so now, at my age? You want to
know why I've stopped putting out your socks and
shirts and handkerchiefs? I did used to enjoy doing
it . . . I know that when a wife lays out a clean shirt
for her husband, it is as if she is saying, "Okay I
should touch your linen and you should let no one
else touch it, because you love me as much as I love
you." Well something happened that made me stop
doing it. I don't even know the reason. One of those
things a woman does and she can't explain why. I'm
not beautiful Peppino. I'm not young. But I'm still a
woman.

PEPPINO. (*Puts his hand over hers.*) You say you
are not beautiful, Rosi'. I was looking at you then
while you were talking. You can't imagine what I saw
in your eyes when you said you loved me. Why
shouldn't I be jealous if another man looks at you and
sees what I see. I used to think when we got married
I should be less jealous. I think I must have married
you partly for that reason.

ROSA. Do you remember the day we were married?
No, you're a man—you don't remember anything, but
after the ceremony, coming down the steps from the
church there were two girls. They were waiting for
another wedding. As we passed them I heard one say,
"Oh look there. The bride's not much, but the bride-
groom's lovely." That was the best wedding present I
could have had. You wore a blue suit and a grey tie,
and I can still remember the shirt you were wearing,
and I looked at you as we passed those girls, and I
can remember thinking, "Yes, he *is* a handsome groom,
but Madonna Mia he's married me so I can't be all

that ugly." (VIRGINIA *comes in Up Right with tray.* MEME *comes in Up Right with six soup bowls.*)

MEME. Nothing gets put away until it's been counted. Go bring the rest of the plates and the big dishes. (VIRGINIA *goes out Up Right.*)

PEPPINO. Amelia, do you mind? Rosa and I are having a private talk. Could you come back in a little while?

MEME. Of course! There's plenty to be getting on with in the kitchen. (MEME *goes out Up Right.*)

PEPPINO. Well then?

ROSA. Well what?

PEPPINO. If you don't want to tell me why you changed, you don't have to, but there is one other thing. Yesterday when you were angry you said one thing that really hit me. You took Roberto in your arms and you said to him, "Robe, it is a miracle that you and I are still alive." What did you mean—it's a miracle that you are both alive? (MEME *with six bowls follows* VIRGINIA *with ten plates.*)

MEME. Put them with the other things, down there. And don't bother the Signor and the Signora again this morning unless I tell you to. They don't want to be disturbed. We've finished now, you can carry on. (MEME *and* VIRGINIA *go out Up Right.* PEPPINO *continues as if there had been not an interruption.*)

PEPPINO. Why did you say it, Rosi'? What did you mean?

ROSA. Can't we talk about it tonight?

PEPPINO. No, now, please, Rosi'.

ROSA. (*She shakes her head slowly, fixing her eyes on him reproachfully.*) You don't remember anything, do you?

PEPPINO. What don't I remember?

ROSA. Let me refresh your memory. Before we were married, the night we had dinner at the Red House in Torre del Greco.

PEPPINO. You asked me that yesterday. Of course I remember. I remember it perfectly.

Rosa. And the reason why you took me there? Do you remember that for five months you had been making love to me and all that time you were engaged to someone else.

Peppino. Yes, to the widow.

Rosa. To the widow. Yes. To the widow.

Peppino. She was a terrible woman that widow. She really made me jump through the hoop.

Rosa. And what did you do to me, Peppi'? What did you put me through?

Peppino. Nothing. I was always frank and honest with you, Rosi'. I told you about the widow, if not the first time we met, the second.

Rosa. Yes, you were honest with me, Peppi'. You told me you were engaged to someone else, and that you could never marry me, but all the same, one night I let you make love to me. Do you remember? "Think what you are doing, Rosi'" you said "I'm already engaged to her" and I said I didn't care because I loved you Peppi', and that was the only thing in the world for me. I didn't want to lose you. I had to make myself a rival to that widow, so I said "It doesn't matter. It's my own business. If I'm happy then I can't complain, whatever happens" and for five months we went on meeting secretly and then you asked me to dinner at the Torre del Greco.

Peppino. Yes, I remember. To tell you that I would have to give up seeing you, because somehow the widow had heard about you. I didn't know how to tell you.

Rosa. You managed it finally and you told me it was the last time I would ever see you.

Peppino. I expected you to cry, but you didn't. You just sat there Rosi', not moving, like a statue. You said "Very well, if it has to be that way," and to think that I had been terrified that you would cry in front of everybody in the restaurant.

Rosa. You were the one with tears in your eyes.

Peppino. I was shocked Rosa, to think that you

could take it so calmly. I was feeling so upset and you didn't seem to be feeling anything at all. And then, suddenly, I grabbed your hand and I said "Rosi', do you know what is going to happen? You are going to marry me." And you said "But what about the widow?" and I said "It's finished with the widow. It's you. You are the one I must marry."

ROSA. I was pregnant then, Peppino, I was already carrying Roberto.

PEPPINO. Then? That night I asked you to marry me? But Rosi', supposing we hadn't got married. What would have happened if that day I decided to stay with the widow?

ROSA. Then I would have killed myself and Roberto.

PEPPINO. And you say that I am the crazy one? Why didn't you tell me? Wouldn't it have been better to have told me the truth.

ROSA. I didn't want you to marry me just because I was carrying your child. That way you would never have wanted me to put out clean shirts for you.

(*There is a long pause. They look at each other for a long time and with the depth of love that has held them together for so many years. During the Scene, they have learnt a lot about each other and they are closer at this moment than they have ever been before.*)

PEPPINO. How I love you, Rosi'.

ROSA. And I you.

MEME. (*Enters Up Right.*) Can I come in? Have you two finished saying what you have to say?

PEPPINO. Come in, Aunt Meme.

MEME. I'd like to get the plates counted and put away.

ROSA. I'll see to the plates myself. (*And she calls* VIRGINIA, *with a voice that is not the voice of an invalid.*) Virgi!

VIRGINIA. (*Off Up Right.*) Coming!

ROSA. Let's count the plates. (*She begins to count the stacks of plates.*)

MEME. I'll get on with the things in the kitchen.

ROSA. You can get on with the things in your own room. I'll see to the things in my kitchen myself. (MEME *exits Up Right.*)

PEPPINO. Rosi', I have to go to the shop this morning. Rocco's waiting for me. (*He goes Off Down Right for his overcoat. Re-enters.*)

ROSA. Then go along.

PEPPINO. (*He goes Left.*) Will you . . . come out on the balcony?

ROSA. (*Pretended short-temper.*) Go on, go on . . .

PEPPINO. (*As if it was a sudden idea.*) One of these days I'm going to ask you to do something for me . . . something to eat. Something you haven't made for a long time. (*He goes back to bedroom for briefcase.*)

ROSA. What might that be?

PEPPINO. Something you're very good at. (*He comes back on closing briefcase and goes Left.*) Macaroni alla Siciliana with melenzane.

ROSA. (*She counting silverware.*) It's too much bother. It's not one of my specialities anyway. If you want Macaroni alla Siciliana, ask Maria Carolina. She does it better than anybody.

PEPPINO. Do you think that Maria Carolina can make Macaroni alla Siciliana?

ROSA. Don't you remember? She cooked it for us one time.

PEPPINO. Did she?

ROSA. You haven't forgotten? You had three platefuls!

PEPPINO. She's your daughter-in-law. I was only trying to encourage her. Didn't I tell you afterwards? It didn't seem to be boiled nearly enough. And the sauce was nowhere as good as yours. (*Kisses her cheek.*)

Rosa. She's still quite young. She has a lot to learn. *Macaroni alla Siciliana!* She's trying to run before she's learnt to walk!

Peppino. Perhaps, one day soon . . . ?

Rosa. Perhaps.

Peppino. I don't mean today. Just think about it. Then, when you feel like cooking it . . .

Rosa. We'll see.

Peppino. I'm going to the shop. (*He goes out Up Left.* Rosa *finishes her arithmetic with the plates and realises that some are missing.* Rosa *starts counting, stops, goes up to balcony.*)

Rosa. Virgi! Are there anymore plates in the kitchen?

Virginia. (*She enters Up Right.*) No, signora.

Rosa. There are two plates missing.

Virginia. There can't be.

Rosa. Do you think I can't do simple arithmetic? (*Calling.*) Amelia!

Meme. (*Offstage.*) What is it?

Rosa. Are there any more plates in the kitchen?

Meme. (*Off.*) No.

Rosa. They've been broken then. (*To* Virginia.) That's your brother's fault! I told you not to let him wash them.

Virginia. He didn't break any, signora. I was standing watching him.

Rosa. I should never use the plates from my best dinner service, Christmas, Easter or any other day I always say the same and I always make the same mistake and they get broken.

Virginia. Signora, it wasn't—

Rosa. And don't interrupt when I'm talking to you. Wait. (Rosa, *remembering* Peppino, *rushes over to the balcony to watch him turn the corner. As* Rosa *starts Upstage:*)

CURTAIN

CURTAIN CALLS

MICHELE enters Up Left with lace tablecloth, goes Down Left, bows same time as Virginia.

VIRGINIA enters Up Right, goes Down Right, bows same time as Michele.

Then Michele and Virginia lay table cloth. When finished, Michele sets plates and Virginia puts pasta bowls on top of plates.

CATIELLE enters Down Left, goes Center, bows with Cefercola.

CEFERCOLA enters Down Right, goes Center, bows with Catielle.

Then Catielle goes Up Left, gets straight chair and sets it at the Up Left end of table.

Cefercola goes off Down Left, brings on bentwood arm chair and puts it at the Left end of the table.

ATTILIO enters Down Left, goes Center, bows with Roberto and Maria.

ROBERTO and MARIA enter Down Right, go Center, bow with Attilio.

Roberto goes Up Right, gets straight chair and sets it at the Up Right end of table. Rocco gives him a decanter and he pours wine on the Downstage side of table.

Maria sets the glasses on the table from the tray which Attilio carries.

Attilio carries tray of wine glasses and follows Maria.

FEDERICO enters Down Left, carrying flowers, goes Center, bows with Rocco and Giulianella.

ROCCO and GIULIANELLA enter Down Right, go Center, bow with Federico. Giulianella and Federico kiss.

Rocco exits Up Right, gets two decanters, hands one to Roberto. Rocco pours wine in Upstage glasses.

Federico gets napkins from small table, sets napkins at big table.

Giulianella gets flowers from small table and puts them in Center of big table. Gets forks from small table and puts one at each place setting, Right end.

ELENA enters Down Left, goes Center, bows with Luigi.
LUIGI enters Down Right, goes Center, bows with Elena.
Elena sets forks on the Stage Left end of table.

RAFFAELE enters Down Left, goes Center, switches side and bows Right of Meme.
MEME enters Down Right, goes Center, switches side and bows Left of Raffaele.
Meme greeted by Cefercola.
Raffaele greeted by Attilio.
ANTONIO enters Down Right, goes Center, bows, shows audience red lining of new jacket. Michele goes to his Right, takes off his cap, Antonio takes it and goes Left. Michele follows.

PEPPINO enters Down Left, goes Center, kisses Rosa, bow together.
ROSA enters Down Right, goes Center, kisses Peppino, bow together.
CURTAIN: IN
EVERYONE sits.

When set—CURTAIN: OUT
Downstage Actors turn and toast the audience.
MEME, LUIGI and RAFFAELE rise, toast audience. Sit again.
ANTONIO rises, toasts audience. Sits again.
PEPPINO and ROSA rise, toast audience. Remain standing.

If there is a THIRD CURTAIN CALL:
Downstage Actors turn and toast the audience.
LUIGI, ROSA, PEPPINO, MEME and ANTONIO rise and toast the audience and remain standing.

PROPERTY LIST

ACT ONE—*On Stage:*
  chair—Downstage of Antonio's table, on Stage floor
  clock—stopped at 5:05, on wall, Down Right over chair
  table—on right wagon, *with:*
    flat iron, Left side of table
    white tin pan *with:*
      rolled cloth, Center of table
    brush—Right side of table
    small iron stand with handle—Left side
    cover over top of table
    on bottom shelf:
      brim forms
      irons
  apron—on wire, on wall over Antonio's table
  shelf over table *with:*
    hat blocks
    hat stretching block
  stool—Upstage of table, on wagon
  stove—Left of table
  garbage can—Right of sink *with:*
    plastic bucket in bottom
  sink—*on wall:*
    assorted pots and pans, ragu pan
  drainboard area—Right of sink:
    dish rack *with:*
      3 soup bowls—Downstage
      4 plates—Upstage
      3 glasses—Right
      10 pieces silverware—Downstage
    rubber gloves—Right of rack
    pot—Upstage of rack
  area Left of sink:
    empty cup
    saucer with 6 garlic slivers
    plate of chopped parsley
    3 sprigs of parsley
    2 plates stacked
    lid to ragu pan
    dry wash cloth

Right drawer:
  cheese grater—handle facing Downstage
Left drawer:
  syringe box—*on top:*
    razor blade under lock
  inside:
    syringe
    needle
    plunger
  gauze pad—under syringe box
  white cloth—under gauze pad
Right cabinet:
  top shelf—tray *with:*
    ziti—on bottom
    bread basket *with:*
      cut bread, top of ziti
    wedge of cheese—on top of ziti
      Downstage of bread
Left cabinet:
  top shelf:
    white bowl (make sure no ziti is in bowl)
hanging from pegs—Left of sink:
  3 aprons
  1 dish towel
chair—Upstage of stove unit
coal bucket *with:*
  coal
  small shovel
  larger shovel
Stove *with:*
  pot on Upstage burner *with:*
    minestrone
    ladle
  2 hot pads—Upstage corner
  fan—Upstage of Upstage burner
  bowl of salt—Left of Upstage burner
  bowl of baking soda—Left of Center burner
    (to be used in case of fire)
  hot pad—between Upstage burners—toward Center
  cloth—between Upstage burners—rear of stove
  pepper grinder—Left of middle burner
  wet rag—between Downstage burners—toward Center

copper pot—between Downstage burners—toward rear
fork—Downstage of Downstage burner—toward rear
skillet—Downstage of Downstage burner—rear of stove
metal fork—hanging on wall—above stove
other forks, spoons, etc. hanging on wall above stove
in Downstage burner:
    razor blade
    syringe ready
      for Meme
chair—Downstage of stove
table *with:*
  chopping board *with:*
    chopped onions
    2 whole onions
    chopper
  plate of chopped onions
  2 damp dish rags
  bowl of 12 garlic buds and 6 cut slivers of garlic
  bowl of tomato puree and spoon
  bowl of lard drippings and spoon
  bowl of lard
  copper can with oil—handle facing Upstage
  bottle of wine
  large wooden ladles (2)
  3 knives
  chopping board with ragu meat
  plate with 2 slices of ham
  4 plates—top plate has 3 slices of bacon
  oval meat platter
  piece of lemon
  in Right drawer:
    3 knives
    3 forks
    3 spoons
  in Left drawer:
    pieces of string
    piece of string 78″ long, marked with red and has a slip
      knot
    scissors
chair—Right of table
chair—Left of table
chair—Up Center of table

ACT TWO—*On Stage:*
  arm chair—Down Right
  arm chair—Down Left *with:*
    hat
    sample of suit cloth
  dining table chair—Right, above door
  dining table chair—Left, above door
  12 dining table chairs—
    to go around table
    cardigan on Left chair
  chair—on balcony with blanket
  small table—on balcony *with:*
    newspaper
    bell
  table *with:*
    velvet floral tablecloth
    plastic cover over the velvet
    lace table cloth on top the plastic covering
    2 cruets
    2 water pitchers
    2 dishes with grated Parmesan cheese and spoons
    tray *with:*
      12 water glasses
      12 wine glasses
    12 knives, 12 forks, 12 spoons
    piece of black wrapping cloth—Down Left end
    sleeve from jacket—on top of black wrapping cloth
    ash tray—Up Left end
    2 salt shakers, 2 pepper shakers

ACT THREE—*On Stage:*
  Strike—
    everything from table, except velvet tablecloth
    fold lace tablecloth accordion style and strike to Off Left
    plastic covering on table
    box and tie from Down Right arm chair
    purse, books, newspaper, eye glasses from Left chair
    gray blanket from balcony chair
    bell, macaroni bowl and glass from balcony table
    4 pieces of jewelry Down Left
    magazine Down Left on floor

Set—
    tray on table—Up Left end *with:*
        2 demitasse cups and saucers
        2 spoons
        sugar bowl
        small coffee pot
    book—Right of tray on table
    pad of paper—Right of tray on table
    pencil—Right of tray on table
    Peppino's briefcase should be Down Right for this Act
Set Off Left:
    folded lace table cloth (accordion style) for curtain call
    for prop men to carry on for curtain call—table *with:*
        lace table cloth
        tray *with:*
            15 wine glasses
            5 dinner plates
            5 forks
            3 pasta bowls
            15 napkins
    refill wine decanters and have them set Off Right for
    curtain calls

END OF SHOW—*On Stage:*
    Strike:
        pillow and blanket from Down Right chair to Off Stage
        tray with mineral water and glass from table to Off Stage
        pad and pencil from table to Off Stage
        tray with silverware from table to Off Stage
    Set:
        10 dinner plates from table to small table Up Stage
        12 pasta bowls from table to small table Up Stage
        table from Off Left to Up Center

ACT ONE—*Off Left:*
GIULIANELLA:
    paper bag with fabric samples, dye envelopes; magazines,
        shoulder bag
LUIGI:
    paper shopping bag with cardboard bottom, olives in plastic
        bag, capers in plastic bag, pine nuts in plastic bag,
        calamari pot with lid, calamari cone with stuffing inside

FEDERICO:
  note
ATTILIO:
  paper shopping bag with medicine bottles, cotton, syringe
      vials
  paper shopping bag with stuffing and weight
ROCCO:
  key
PEPPINO:
  key, briefcase with papers, batteries for clock
RAFFAELE:
  clippings
MEME:
  key

ACT TWO—*Off Left:*
FEDERICO:
  flowers—small mums surrounding, 2 large chrysanthemums
MARIA:
  box tied with gold cord with necktie
ROBERTO:
  cassata
LUIGI:
  cassata
GIULIANELLA:
  magazine
MEME:
  newspaper
CEFERCOLA:
  two books
RAFFAELE:
  mask

ACT THREE—*Off Left:*
PEPPINO:
  bunch of keys
GIULIANELLA:
  magazine
CEFERCOLA:
  doctor's bag with stethoscope, bottles, pad, pencil, vials

FEDERICO—Curtain Calls:

bunch of flowers—just the small mums from Act Two
See page 104 for Off Left prop set up for Curtain Calls

ACT ONE—*Off Right:*
VIRGINIA:

door slam, 12 dinner plates

ACT TWO—*Off Right:*
VIRGINIA:

11 pasta bowls; 11 napkins; 12 dinner plates (6 plates, then a napkin, then 6 plates); 3 wine decanters with wine; pitcher of wine with funnel; glass of water for Antonio; bowl with macaroni and cheese; green salad and spoon; omelette with napkin, knife, fork; plate with mozzarella, 6 green olives, knife, fork, glass of water; pasta bowl with pasta and ladle; bread basket with bread

ROBERTO:

piece of bread, small bowl of sauce

MARIA:

omelette, knife, napkin, fork

MICHELE:

bowl of flowers

RAFFAELE:

tambourine

MEME:

syringe—double from Act One

ACT THREE—*Off Right:*
MEME:

glass of orange juice

VIRGINIA:

glass of orange juice; 5 breakfast plates, 5 knives, 5 forks, 5 napkins; tray with 8 cups, 6 saucers, coffee pot, sugar, creamer, doily; tray with silverware from Act Two, pad of paper and pencil; 12 pasta bowls; 10 dinner plates; tray with glass—mineral water; meat platter with meat fork; bread basket with bread

ATTILIO:

red blanket and pillow

PEPPINO:

briefcase from Act One